The Official PGP User's Guide

The Official PGP User's Guide

Philip Zimmermann

The MIT Press, Cambridge, Massachusetts, and London, England

This book was set in New Baskerville and Courier at The MIT Press and was printed and bound in the United States of America.

Library of Congress Cataloging-in-Publication Data

Zimmermann, Philip (Philip R.)
  The official PGP user's guide / Philip Zimmermann.
    p.   cm.
  Includes bibliographical references and index.
  ISBN 0-262-74017-6 (pb: alk. paper)
  1. PGP (Computer file) 2. Telecommunication systems—Security measures—Data processing. 3. Electronic mail systems—Security measures—Data processing. 4. Cryptography. I. Title.
TK5102.85.Z56   1995
005.8′2—dc20   95-13653
                                                                            CIP

Contents

Foreword: A Pretty Bad Problem

John Perry Barlow

I love irony, and there lies in this book an irony as striking as any I know. It is this: that a computer program with the cute li'l ol' name of Pretty Good Privacy, written by an apparently unformidable gnome on a tight budget, now terrifies a security monolith which required half a century, uncounted billions of dollars, and the collective IQ's of a few thousand geniuses to develop.

This book and the software it describes, as brief and modest as its author, could very well be the root tendril which will grow into the National Security State and shatter it. If that is true, it's probably only a little hyperbolic to claim that you are holding a work as liberating as *Common Sense*, or, viewed through another set of bunker slits, as socially disruptive as *Mein Kampf*.

That doubtless sounds like a pretty disruptive statement itself, but it's not unconsidered. It seems to me that the combination of distributed digital technology and robust encryption has brought informatized society to a very sharp balance point between two lousy choices. On one side lies a technological foundation upon which the most massive totalitarianism could be built. On the other is a jungle in which any number of anarchic guerrillas might hide, upon whom little order could ever be imposed.

Assuming I'm not simply raving here, what leads me to this conclusion? Have things really gotten this weird? I honestly believe they may have.

At present most of us unwittingly leave a highly visible and nearly indelible trail in Cyberspace. Every time we make a modern financial transaction, use the telephone, send an email message, we leave a path of bits from which anyone who's interested and properly equipped can assemble the detailed informational ghosts of our naked selves. If you have something you'd rather hide, don't hide it there.

Furthermore, the tools of surveillance are becoming far more sophisticated and conducive to centralization. Massive pattern recognition engines can be applied to the Net from, say, Washington, DC, or Beijing, and specifically tuned to recognize certain kinds of activities. Or even beliefs.

Any government that can automatically generate an intimate profile of every one of its citizens is a government endowed with a potential for absolute power that will eventually, to use Lord Acton's phrase, corrupt absolutely. Few civil liberties are likely to survive such capacities in the hands of the increasingly panicky authoritarians who run the embattled old bureaucracies of the Meat World.

Worse, their panic may be justified. An equally apprehensive and growing lot of cyber-libertarians now have at their disposal tools as unbalancingly powerful in their power to conceal as are the other side's in the service of revelation. One of these sabots goes by the mild name of Pretty Good Privacy.

Any number of citizens armed with PGP and such of its relations as digital cash and anonymous Net remailers can simply vanish from the governmental radar. They are at greater liberty than ever before to conduct any endeavor, including something which, as Phil frankly puts it at the beginning of this book, "shouldn't be illegal, but is." They can exempt themselves from taxes and yet maintain precise accounting records. In many ways, they can effectively resign from the community of the governed and enter a condition in which their actions are ordered by conscience and culture alone.

And we may get a chance to find out just how well these are going to work as the primary templates for social order. There is no question that the patterns of unwritten code which arise from culture can work when the society in question is small, simple, or highly homogeneous.

For example, I come from a part of Wyoming where something like the Code of the West is still more important than the law or its instruments. It works pretty well. I don't have a key to my house, and through many years in the cattle business, I signed few contracts and was never knowingly cheated.

Something similar obtains in Japan, a much larger and more complex society which is nevertheless monocultural enough to resist chaos far more by general consent than by any order which police might enforce. And it is nearly crime free.

The emergent social orders of both Japan and Wyoming strongly support the idea that a less legalistic approach to the vicissitudes of life among the humans will work. What it less well known is whether it is possible to return to such a condition and whether truly diverse societies, such as we have in America, can be ordered primarily by cultural norms.

Present evidence from both the Former Soviet Union and the Former Yugoslavia is not so promising. After 70 years of the most heroic efforts to force order by imposed regulation, the great iron lid is off. And it is no Rousseauvian paradise to which the Russians have returned. They appear to be governed less by ethics than by criminals who would probably govern better if they were organized. Meanwhile the Balkans have returned to a state of tribal bloodshed which indicates that a strong sense of community, as expressed in cultural immune response, can be more disruptive than ordering.

But what are the choices? Do we allow matters to continue along their present technological trajectory, eventually endowing our government (and practically any marketing organization) with a magnifying window into the least of our lives? Do we allow ourselves to become intimately vulnerable to faceless bureaucracies to whom we will be incredibly well known yet remain faceless ourselves? We have gone too far that way already. But what can prevent a further tumble toward that dark horizon?

Do we try to hide our trails behind laws (favored by Europeans) which would define what might be the appropriate contents for a database? Do we endow government with the ability to define forbidden knowledge? I don't have much enthusiasm for this solution, which sounds to me rather like having a peeping tom install one's window blinds. I do not trust government with the ability to regulate information, especially information which contains within it such a long lever of control as those things about yourself you'd rather no one knew.

There are always special circumstances—grave matters of national security, they will insist—in which it will seem obvious to our guardians that the sanctity of such laws is secondary to the greater public interest. Indeed, this is how we have been doing things in America for a long time. The Bill of Rights continues to apply only when the government feels no pain from its application.

It's a tough choice, but I think I would prefer to give people the means to control their own information. I would prefer to let my fellow citizens detach their economic transactions from their identities, despite the looming possibility that an anonymous economy will consider taxes voluntary. I would even rather extend to people the general condition of anonymity, hoping they will not use it much, knowing that without identity, there is little impetus for responsibility, and that without responsibility, the Social Contract is abrogated.

While I have focused so far on the ability of PGP to conceal, it is in the area of identity that this software may make its most positive contribution. Even as digital technology can make us too visible, the absence of real bodies places a garment of ambiguity on everyone who interacts on the Net. If community requires identity, what is to be done about the ease with which the virtual can take on somebody else's identity?

To this dilemma, PGP provides an unambiguous solution: digital signature. Using the signing techniques enabled here, you can send and receive files with great assurance that they were generated by their purported authors and that their contents have not been altered. Once you are in the habit of authenticating your own words, no one may pretend to speak or act as you. You can be assured that you will only have to be responsible for your own actions and not the misdeeds of some phantom wearing your name.

For the rest of what PGP enables, ambivalence is the only appropriate response. Still, I would at least rather everyone know how to use the tools whose operation this book describes, though I fervently hope they will be somewhat circumspect about actually using them. Just as an armed populace may be more resistant to certain excesses of governmental zeal, so might a populace armed with the ultimate defensive weapon, the ability to disappear, countervail against the all-seeing electronic eye.

We had best be armed with something. Because it seems certain to me that any government which can see everything we do all the time will sooner or later feel compelled to add omnipotence to omniscience, which are, in the Virtual Age, much the same thing anyway.

Maybe we will feel compelled to start using them. Maybe there will be anarchy, maybe even chaos. But chaos at least has an open architecture. Chaos has always been the native home of the infinitely possible. And among the possibilities I imagine is that human beings will turn out to be better, less paranoid, less worthy of inspiring paranoia, than many of us think.

In the end, it doesn't matter much what they think or I think. The genie of guerrilla cryptography is out of the bottle. Even Phil Zimmermann, the Ali Baba who rubbed this particular lamp, can't stuff it back in or keep it within what America laughably calls its borders. The genie is all over the Net. It's in your hands as you hold this book. Summon it with a conscience. But be prepared to summon it if you must.

Preface

This book is about a software package called Pretty Good Privacy, or PGP, which has become the worldwide de facto standard for email encryption. This book explains how to use PGP, but it also gives a brief introduction to the politics and technology of cryptography in general and to public key cryptography in particular.

PGP is available as freeware on the Internet, including an ASCII version of this manual. You can read it on your computer screen. But I find that it's always better to have user documentation on my desk, nicely typeset and bound, in a form I can read without sitting in front of a computer. If you use PGP, you should buy this book.

The book is divided into two parts. The first contains the essential topics all PGP users need to read, while the second contains special topics for power users. People often complain about computer manuals being so big, so intimidating for novices. I have tried to make this one brief, leaving out the minutiae of the program, to make it more approachable.

Cryptography software involves trust—trust in the algorithms, trust in the protocols, trust in the way keys are managed, trust in the integrity of the implementor. Somehow, PGP and I both have become widely trusted by PGP users. Part of the reason is that I published the source code to PGP so that people can inspect it for "back doors," so that they don't have to trust me. And part of the reason comes from the informal style in which this manual is written, which seems to strike a chord with many users. I get a lot of email about this. One PGP user told me that this is the first computer manual he'd seen that should be read aloud. In its electronic form, this manual has already introduced thousands of people to cryptography, and many say that it has shaken their faith in most other commercial cryptographic products.

Cryptography used to be an obscure science, of little relevance to everyday life. Historically, it always had a special role in military and diplomatic communications. But in the Information Age, cryptography is about political power, and in particular, about the power relationship between a government and its people. It is about the right to privacy, freedom of speech, freedom of political association, freedom of the press, freedom from unreasonable search and seizure, freedom to be left alone. Citizen use of cryptography seems to be on a collision course with the self-proclaimed needs of the police, both the well-intentioned police of democratic states and the brutal security forces of police states, because it tips the scales in favor of the individual's rights.

In the three years since PGP was published, much has happened to confirm our fears of government power. The U.S. federal government wants to build a nationwide communication system designed for domestic surveillance, with technologies that in the long run can be used by the tyrants of the world to keep themselves in power.

In those three years, PGP has spread like a prairie fire, becoming popular throughout the world, over a broad political spectrum that includes human rights workers, civil libertarians, college students, gay activists, religious fundamentalists, leftists, cowboy computer entrepreneurs, journalists, political activists of all stripes, and free-thinking people. It has helped protect the disempowered from the powerful. It has become a seed crystal for the growth of the Crypto Revolution, a new political movement for civil liberties in the Information Age. And I have come under criminal investigation for unleashing such a powerful piece of free software on the world.

How could all this have happened, from just sitting at home and writing a little piece of software modestly called "Pretty Good Privacy"? Well, read this book and get the software, and find out just how much political power can be embodied in a computer program.

Boulder, Colorado
October 1994

Acknowledgments

Formidable obstacles and powerful forces have been arrayed to stop PGP. Dedicated people are helping to overcome these obstacles. PGP has achieved notoriety as "underground software," and bringing PGP "above ground" as fully licensed freeware has required patience and persistence. I'd especially like to thank Hal Abelson, Jeff Schiller, Brian LaMacchia, and Derek Atkins at MIT for their determined efforts. I'd also like to thank Jim Bruce and David Litster in the MIT administration and Bob Prior and Terry Ehling at The MIT Press. And I'd like to thank my entire legal defense team, whose job is not over yet. I used to tell a lot of lawyer jokes, before I encountered so many positive examples of lawyers in my legal defense team, most of whom work pro bono.

The development of PGP has turned into a social phenomenon whose political appeal has inspired the collective efforts of an ever-growing number of volunteer programmers. Remember that children's story called "Stone Soup"?

I'd like to thank the following people for their contributions to the creation of Pretty Good Privacy. Although I was the author of PGP version 1.0, major parts of later versions of PGP were implemented by an international collaborative effort involving a large number of contributors, under my design guidance.

Branko Lankester, Hal Finney, and Peter Gutmann all contributed a huge amount of time adding features for PGP 2.0 and porting it to Unix variants. Hugh Kennedy ported it to VAX/VMS, Lutz Frank ported it to the Atari ST, and Cor Bosman and Colin Plumb ported it to the Commodore Amiga.

Translation of PGP into foreign languages was done by Jean-loup Gailly in France, Armando Ramos in Spain, Felipe Rodriquez Svensson and Branko Lankester in The Netherlands, Miguel Angel Gallardo in Spain, Hugh Kennedy and Lutz Frank in Germany, David Vincenzetti in Italy, Harry Bush and Maris Gabalins in Latvia, Zygimantas Cepaitis in Lithuania, Peter Suchkow and Andrew Chernov in Russia, and Alexander Smishlajev in Esperantujo. Peter Gutmann offered to translate it into New Zealand English, but we finally decided PGP could get by with U.S. English.

Jean-loup Gailly, Mark Adler, and Richard B. Wales published the ZIP compression code and granted permission for its inclusion in PGP. The MD5 routines were developed and placed in the public domain by Ron Rivest. The IDEA™ cipher was developed by Xuejia Lai and James L. Massey at ETH in Zurich and is used in PGP with permission from Ascom-Tech AG.

Charlie Merritt originally taught me how to do decent multiprecision arithmetic for public key cryptography, and Jimmy Upton contributed a faster multiply/modulo algorithm. Thad Smith implemented an even faster modmult algorithm. Zhahai Stewart contributed a lot of useful ideas on PGP file formats and other stuff, including having more than one user ID for a key. I heard the idea of introducers from Whit Diffie. Kelly Goen did most of the work for the initial electronic publication of PGP 1.0.

Various contributions of coding effort also came from Colin Plumb, Derek Atkins, and Castor Fu. Other contributions of effort, coding or otherwise, have come from Hugh Miller, Eric Hughes, Tim May, Stephan Neuhaus, and many others. Zbigniew Fiedorowicz did the first Macintosh port.

Since the release of PGP 2.0, many programmers have sent in patches and bug fixes and porting adjustments for other computers. My thanks go to all of them.

Just as in the Stone Soup story, it is getting harder to peer through the thick soup to see the stone at the bottom of the pot that I dropped in to start it all off.

Note for Macintosh Users

PGP was originally developed for MSDOS and Unix machines, and this manual is written for these implementations, which use a command-line interface for all PGP functions. There does exist a Macintosh version of the program, though, in which all these functions are accessed through pull-down menus and dialog boxes. There is also on-line help for using MacPGP, and there should be some Mac-specific user documentation included in the MacPGP release package, in addition to this manual.

Almost all good Mac software applications are written from scratch, not ported there from other operating systems. The current Mac version of PGP was ported by Zbigniew Fiedorowicz. Since the MSDOS/Unix version of PGP was not designed for a graphical user interface (GUI), this was not an easy task, and many bugs still remain. An all-new version of PGP, designed for easy adaptation to a GUI, is under development, and a new Mac version will be developed from this new PGP source code. It will be more Mac-like and more reliable. Despite the bugs in the current version of MacPGP, however, it is important to note that if Zbigniew had waited for this new version to be developed before he created MacPGP, the world would have been deprived of a Mac version of the program for far too long.

I
Essential Topics

Quick Overview

Pretty Good™ Privacy (PGP), from Phil's Pretty Good Software, is a high security cryptographic software application for MSDOS, Unix, VAX/VMS, and other computers. PGP allows people to exchange files or messages with privacy, authentication, and convenience. Privacy means that only those intended to receive a message can read it. Authentication means that messages that appear to be from a particular person can only have originated from that person. Convenience means that privacy and authentication are provided without the hassles of managing keys associated with conventional cryptographic software. No secure channels are needed to exchange keys between users, and this makes PGP much easier to use. This is because PGP is based on a powerful new technology called "public key" cryptography.

PGP combines the convenience of the Rivest-Shamir-Adleman (RSA) public key cryptosystem with the speed of conventional cryptography, message digests for digital signatures, data compression before encryption, good ergonomic design, and sophisticated key management. And PGP performs the public key functions faster than most other software implementations. PGP is public key cryptography for the masses.

PGP does not provide any built-in modem communications capability. You must use a separate software product for that.

Part I explains the essential concepts for using PGP and should be read by all users. Part II covers the advanced features of PGP and other special topics and should be read by serious users. Neither part explains the underlying technological details of cryptographic algorithms and data structures.

For detailed information on PGP licensing, distribution, copyrights, patents, trademarks, liability limitations, and export controls, see chapter 12.

1

Why Do You Need PGP?

"Whatever you do will be insignificant, but it is very important that you do it."
—Mahatma Gandhi

It's personal. It's private. And it's no one's business but yours. You may be planning a political campaign, discussing your taxes, or having an illicit affair. Or you may be doing something that you feel shouldn't be illegal, but is. Whatever it is, you don't want your private electronic mail (email) or confidential documents read by anyone else. There's nothing wrong with asserting your privacy. Privacy is as apple-pie as the Constitution.

Perhaps you think your email is legitimate enough that encryption is unwarranted. If you really are a law-abiding citizen with nothing to hide, then why don't you always send your paper mail on postcards? Why not submit to drug testing on demand? Why require a warrant for police searches of your house? Are you trying to hide something? You must be a subversive or a drug dealer if you hide your mail inside envelopes. Or maybe a paranoid nut. Do law-abiding citizens have any need to encrypt their email?

What if everyone believed that law-abiding citizens should use postcards for their mail? If some brave soul tried to assert his or her privacy by using an envelope, it would draw suspicion. Perhaps the authorities would open the mail to see what is being hidden. Fortunately, we don't live in that kind of world, because everyone protects most of their mail with envelopes. So no one draws suspicion by asserting their privacy with an envelope. There is safety in numbers. Analogously, it would be nice if everyone routinely used encryption for all their email, innocent or not, so that no one drew suspicion by asserting their email privacy with encryption. Think of it as a form of solidarity.

Today, if the government wants to violate the privacy of ordinary citizens, it has to expend a certain amount of expense and labor to intercept and steam open and read paper mail and listen to and possibly transcribe spoken telephone conversation. This kind of labor-intensive monitoring is not practical on a large scale. It is only done in important cases when it seems worthwhile.

More and more of our private communications are being routed through electronic channels. Electronic mail is gradually replacing conventional paper mail. Email messages are just too easy to intercept and scan for interesting keywords. This can be done easily, routinely, automatically, and undetectably on a grand scale. International cablegrams are already scanned this way on a large scale by the National Security Agency (NSA).

We are moving toward a future in which the nation will be crisscrossed with high capacity fiber optic data networks linking together all our increasingly ubiquitous personal computers. Email will be the norm for everyone, not the novelty it is today. The government will protect our email with government-designed encryption protocols. Probably most people will acquiesce to that. But perhaps some people will prefer their own protective measures.

Senate Bill 266, a 1991 omnibus anticrime bill, had an unsettling measure buried in it. If this nonbinding resolution had become law, it would have forced manufacturers of secure communications equipment to insert special "trap doors" in their products, so that the government could read anyone's encrypted messages. It read: "It is the sense of Congress that providers of electronic communications services and manufacturers of electronic communications service equipment shall insure that communications systems permit the Government to obtain the plain text contents of voice, data, and other communications when appropriately authorized by law." This measure was defeated after rigorous protest from civil libertarians and industry groups.

In 1992, the FBI Digital Telephony wiretap proposal was introduced to Congress. It would require all manufacturers of communications equipment to build in special remote wiretap ports that would enable the FBI to wiretap all forms of electronic communication from FBI offices. Although it never attracted any sponsors in Congress in 1992 because of citizen opposition, it was reintroduced and passed in 1994.

Most alarming of all is the White House's bold new encryption policy initiative, under development at NSA since the start of the Bush administration and unveiled on April 16, 1993. The centerpiece of this initiative is a government-built encryption device, called the "Clipper" chip, containing a new classified NSA encryption algorithm. The government is encouraging private industry to design it into all their secure communication products, such as secure phones and secure FAX machines. AT&T is now putting the Clipper into their secure voice products. The catch: At the time of manufacture, each Clipper chip will be loaded with its own unique key, and the government gets to keep a copy, placed in escrow. Not to worry, though—the government promises that they will use these keys to read your traffic only when duly authorized by law. Of course, to make Clipper completely effective, the next logical step would be to outlaw other forms of cryptography.

If privacy is outlawed, only outlaws will have privacy. Intelligence agencies have access to good cryptographic technology. So do the big arms and drug traffickers. So do defense contractors, oil companies, and other corporate giants. But ordinary people and grassroots political organizations mostly have not had access to affordable "military grade" public key cryptographic technology. Until now.

PGP empowers people to take their privacy into their own hands. There's a growing social need for it. That's why I wrote it.

2

How Public Key Cryptography Works

It would help if you were already familiar with the concept of cryptography in general and public key cryptography in particular. For those of you who are not, here is a very brief introduction to public key cryptography.

First, some elementary terminology. Suppose I want to send you a message, but I don't want anyone but you to be able to read it. I can *encrypt*, or *encipher*, the message, which means I scramble it up in a hopelessly complicated way, rendering it unreadable to anyone except you, the intended recipient of the message. I supply a cryptographic *key* to encrypt the message, and you have to use the same key to *decipher* or *decrypt* it. At least that's how it works in conventional "single-key" cryptosystems.

In conventional cryptosystems, such as the U.S. Federal Data Encryption Standard (DES), a single key is used for both encryption and decryption. This means that a key must be initially transmitted via secure channels so that both parties can know it before encrypted messages can be sent over insecure channels. This may be inconvenient. If you have a secure channel for exchanging keys, then why do you need cryptography in the first place?

In *public key* cryptosystems, everyone has two related complementary keys, a publicly revealed key and a *secret key* (also frequently called a *private key*). Each key unlocks the code that the other key makes. Knowing the public key does not help you deduce the corresponding secret key. The public key can be published and widely disseminated across a communications network. This protocol provides privacy without the need for the same kind of secure channels that a conventional cryptosystem requires.

Anyone can use a recipient's public key to encrypt a message to that person, and that recipient uses her own corresponding secret key to decrypt that message. No one but the recipient can decrypt it, because no one else has access to that secret key. Not even the person who encrypted the message can decrypt it.

Message authentication is also provided. The sender's own secret key can be used to encrypt a message, thereby signing it. This creates a digital signature of a message, which the recipient (or anyone else) can check by using the sender's public key to decrypt it. This proves that the sender was the true originator of the message, and that the message has not been subsequently altered by anyone else, because the sender alone possesses the secret key that made that signature. Forgery of a signed message is infeasible, and the sender cannot later disavow his signature.

These two processes can be combined to provide both privacy and authentication by first signing a message with your own secret key, then encrypting the signed message with the recipient's public key. The recipient reverses these steps by first decrypting the message with her own secret key, then checking the enclosed signature with your public key. These steps are done automatically by the recipient's software.

Because the public key encryption algorithm is much slower than conventional single-key encryption, encryption is better accomplished by using a high-quality, fast, conventional single-key encryption algorithm to encipher the message. This original unenciphered message is called *plaintext*. In a process invisible to the user, a temporary random key, created just for this one "session," is used to conventionally encipher the plaintext file. Then the recipient's public key is used to encipher this temporary random conventional key. This public-key-enciphered conventional "session" key is sent along with the enciphered text (called *ciphertext*) to the recipient. The recipient uses her own secret key to recover this temporary session key, and then uses that key to run the fast conventional single-key algorithm to decipher the large ciphertext message.

Public keys are kept in key *certificates* that include the key owner's user ID (which is that person's name), a timestamp of when the key pair was generated, and the actual key material. Public key certificates contain the public key material, while secret key certificates contain the secret key material. Each secret key is also encrypted with its own password, in case it gets stolen. A key file, or key ring, contains one or more of these key certificates. Public key rings contain public key certificates, and secret key rings contain secret key certificates.

The keys are also internally referenced by a key *ID*, which is an "abbreviation" of the public key (the least significant 64 bits of the large public key). When this key ID is displayed, only the lower 32 bits are shown for further brevity. While many keys may share the same user ID, for all practical purposes no two keys share the same key ID.

PGP uses message *digests* to form signatures. A message digest is a 128-bit cryptographically strong one-way hash function of the message. It is somewhat analogous to a "checksum" or CRC error checking code, in that it compactly "represents" the message and is used to detect changes in the message. Unlike a CRC, however, it is computationally infeasible for an attacker to devise a substitute message that would produce an identical message digest. The message digest gets encrypted by the secret key to form a signature.

Documents are signed by prefixing them with signature certificates, which contain the key ID of the key that was used to sign it, a secret-key-signed message digest of the document, and a timestamp of when the signature was made. The key ID is used by the receiver to look up the sender's public key to check the signature. The receiver's software automatically looks up the sender's public key and user ID in the receiver's public key ring.

Encrypted files are prefixed by the key ID of the public key used to encrypt them. The receiver uses this key ID message prefix to look up the secret key needed to decrypt the message. The receiver's software automatically looks up the necessary secret decryption key in the receiver's secret key ring.

These two types of key rings are the principal method of storing and managing public and secret keys. Rather than keep individual keys in separate key files, they are collected in key rings to facilitate the automatic lookup of keys either by key ID or by user ID. Each user keeps his own pair of key rings. An individual public key is temporarily kept in a separate file long enough to send to your friend who will then add it to her key ring.

3

Installing PGP

The MSDOS PGP release package comes in a compressed archive file with a file named in this form 'PGPxx.ZIP' (each release version has a different number for the 'xx' in the filename). For example, the release package for version 2.6 is called 'PGP26.ZIP'. The archive can be decompressed with the MSDOS shareware decompression utility PKUNZIP, or the Unix utility unzip. When the PGP release package is decompressed, several files emerge from it. One such file, called 'README.DOC', should always be read before installing PGP. This file contains late-breaking news on what's new in this release of PGP, as well as information on what's in all the other files included in the release.

If you already have an earlier version of PGP, you should rename it or delete it, to avoid name conflicts with the new PGP.

For full details on how to install PGP, see the separate *PGP Installation Guide,* in the file 'SETUP.DOC' included with this release package. It fully describes how to set up the PGP directory and your 'AUTOEXEC.BAT' file and how to use PKUNZIP to install it. We will just briefly summarize the installation instructions here, in case you are too impatient to read the more detailed installation manual right now.

To install PGP on your MSDOS system, you have to copy the compressed archive 'PGPxx.ZIP' file into a suitable directory on your hard disk (like 'C:\PGP'), and decompress it with PKUNZIP. For best results, you should also modify your 'AUTOEXEC.BAT' file, as described elsewhere in this manual, but you can do that later, after you've played with PGP a bit and read more of this manual. If you haven't run PGP before, the first step after installation (and reading this manual) is to make a pair of keys for yourself by running the PGP key generation command pgp -kg. First read the section "RSA Key Generation" in chapter 5.

Installing on Unix and VAX/VMS is generally similar to installing on MSDOS, but you may have to compile the source code first. A Unix makefile is provided with the source release for this purpose.

4

Using PGP

To See a Usage Summary

To see a quick command usage summary for PGP, just type:

```
pgp -h
```

Encrypting a Message

To encrypt a plaintext file with the recipient's public key, type:

```
pgp -e textfile her_userid
```

This command produces a ciphertext file called '*textfile*.pgp'. A specific example is:

```
pgp -e letter.txt Alice
```

or:

```
pgp -e letter.txt "Alice S"
```

The first example searches your public key ring file, 'pubring.pgp', for any public key certificates that contain the string "Alice" anywhere in the user ID field. The second example would find any user IDs that contain "Alice S". You can't use spaces in the string on the command line unless you enclose the whole string in quotes. The search is not case-sensitive. If it finds a matching public key, it uses it to encrypt the plaintext file 'letter.txt', producing a ciphertext file called 'letter.pgp'.

PGP attempts to compress the plaintext before encrypting it, thereby greatly enhancing resistance to cryptanalysis. Thus the ciphertext file will likely be smaller than the plaintext file.

If you want to send this encrypted message through email channels, convert it into printable ASCII "radix-64" format by adding the '-a' option, as described later.

Encrypting a Message to Multiple Recipients

If you want to send the same message to more than one person, you may specify encryption for several recipients, any of whom may decrypt the same ciphertext file. To specify multiple recipients, just add more user IDs to the command line, like so:

```
pgp -e letter.txt Alice Bob Carol
```

This would create a ciphertext file called 'letter.pgp' that could be decrypted by Alice or Bob or Carol. Any number of recipients may be specified.

Signing a Message

To sign a plaintext file with your secret key, type:

```
pgp -s textfile [-u your_userid]
```

Note that '[brackets]' denote an optional field, so don't actually type real brackets.

This command produces a signed file called '*textfile*.pgp'. A specific example is:

```
pgp -s letter.txt -u Bob
```

This searches your secret key ring file 'secring.pgp' for any secret key certificates that contain the string "Bob" anywhere in the user ID field. Your name is Bob, isn't it? The search is not case-sensitive. If it finds a matching secret key, it uses it to sign the plaintext file 'letter.txt', producing a signature file called 'letter.pgp'.

If you leave off the user ID field, the first key on your secret key ring is used as the default secret key for your signature.

PGP attempts to compress the message after signing it. Thus the signed file will likely be smaller than the original file, which is useful for archival applications. However, this renders the file unreadable to the casual human observer, even if the original message was ordinary ASCII text. It would be nice if you could make a signed file that was still directly readable to a human. This would be particularly useful if you want to send a signed message as email.

For signing email messages, where you most likely do want the result to be human-readable, it is probably most convenient to use the CLEARSIG feature. This allows the signature to be applied in printable form at the end of the text and also disables compression of the text. This means the text is still human-readable by the recipient even if the recipient doesn't use PGP to check the signature. This feature is explained in detail in chapter 9. If you can't wait to read that section of the manual, you can see how an email message signed this way would look, with this example:

pgp -sta *message.txt*

This would create a signed message in file '*message*.asc', comprised of the original text, still human-readable, appended with a printable ASCII signature certificate, ready to send through an email system. This example assumes that you are using the normal settings for enabling the CLEARSIG flag in the config file.

Signing and Then Encrypting

To sign a plaintext file with your secret key and then encrypt it with the recipient's public key, type:

pgp -es *textfile her_userid* [-u *your_userid*]

Note that '[brackets]' denote an optional field, so don't actually type real brackets.

This example produces a nested ciphertext file that is called
'*textfile*.pgp'. Your secret key to create the signature is automatically
looked up in your secret key ring via *your_userid*. Her public
encryption key is automatically looked up in your public key ring
via *her_userid*. If you leave off her user ID field from the command
line, you will be prompted for it.

If you leave off your own user ID field, the first key on your secret
key ring is be used as the default secret key for your signature.

Note that PGP attempts to compress the plaintext before encrypting it.

If you want to send this encrypted message through email channels, convert it into printable ASCII "radix-64" format by adding
the '-a' option, as described later.

Multiple recipients may be specified by adding more user IDs to
the command line.

Using Conventional Encryption

Sometimes you just need to encrypt a file the old-fashioned way,
with conventional single-key cryptography. This approach is useful
for protecting archive files that will be stored but will not be sent to
anyone else. Since the same person that encrypted the file will also
decrypt the file, public key cryptography is not really necessary.

To encrypt a plaintext file with just conventional cryptography,
type:

```
pgp -c textfile
```

This example encrypts the plaintext file called *textfile*, producing a
ciphertext file called '*textfile*.pgp', without using public key cryptography, key rings, user IDs, or any of that stuff. It prompts you for
a pass phrase to use as a conventional key to encipher the file. This
pass phrase need not be (and, indeed, should not be) the same pass
phrase that you use to protect your own secret key. Note that PGP
attempts to compress the plaintext before encrypting it.

PGP will not encrypt the same plaintext the same way twice, even
if you used the same pass phrase every time.

Decrypting and Checking Signatures

To decrypt an encrypted file, or to check the signature integrity of
a signed file:

pgp *ciphertextfile* [-o *plaintextfile*]

Note that '[brackets]' denote an optional field, so don't actually type real brackets.

The ciphertext file name is assumed to have a default extension
of '.pgp'. The optional plaintext output file name specifies where
to put processed plaintext output. If no name is specified, the
ciphertext filename is used, with no extension. If a signature is
nested inside of an encrypted file, it is automatically decrypted and
the signature integrity is checked. The full user ID of the signer is
displayed.

Note that the "unwrapping" of the ciphertext file is completely
automatic, regardless of whether the ciphertext file is just signed,
just encrypted, or both. PGP uses the key ID prefix in the ciphertext
file to automatically find the appropriate secret decryption key on
your secret key ring. If there is a nested signature, PGP then uses
the key ID prefix in the nested signature to automatically find the
appropriate public key on your public key ring to check the
signature. If all the right keys are already present on your key rings,
no user intervention is required, except that you will be prompted
for your password for your secret key if necessary. If the ciphertext
file was conventionally encrypted without public key cryptography,
PGP recognizes this and prompts you for the pass phrase to
conventionally decrypt it.

5

Managing Keys

Since the time of Julius Caesar, key management has always been the hardest part of cryptography. One of the principal distinguishing features of PGP is its sophisticated key management.

RSA Key Generation

To generate your own unique public/secret key pair of a specified size, type:

```
pgp -kg
```

PGP shows you a menu of recommended key sizes (low commercial grade, high commercial grade, or "military" grade) and prompts you for what size key you want, up to more than a thousand bits. The bigger the key, the more security you get, but you pay a price in speed.

It also asks for a user ID, which means your name. It's a good idea to use your full name as your user ID, because then there is less risk of other people using the wrong public key to encrypt messages to you. Spaces and punctuation are allowed in the user ID. It would help if you put your email address in <angle brackets> after your name, like so:

```
Robert M Smith <rms@xyzcorp.com>
```

If you don't have an email address, use your phone number or some other unique information that would help ensure that your user ID is unique.

PGP also asks for a pass phrase to protect your secret key in case it falls into the wrong hands. Nobody can use your secret key file without this pass phrase. The *pass phrase* is like a password, except that it can be a whole phrase or sentence with many words, spaces, punctuation, or anything else you want in it. Don't lose this pass phrase—there is no way to recover it if you do lose it. This pass phrase will be needed later every time you use your secret key. The pass phrase is case-sensitive and should not be too short or easy to guess. It is never displayed on the screen. Don't leave it written down anywhere where someone else can see it, and don't store it on your computer. If you don't want a pass phrase (You fool!), just press return (or enter) at the pass phrase prompt.

The public/secret key pair is derived from large truly random numbers derived mainly from measuring the intervals between your keystrokes with a fast timer. The software will ask you to enter some random text to help it accumulate some random bits for the keys. When asked, you should provide some keystrokes that are reasonably random in their timing, and it wouldn't hurt to make the actual characters that you type irregular in content as well. Some of the randomness is derived from the unpredictability of the content of what you type. So don't just type repeated sequences of characters.

Note that RSA key generation is a lengthy process. It may take a few seconds for a small key on a fast processor, or quite a few minutes for a large key on an old IBM PC/XT. PGP will visually indicate its progress during key generation.

The generated key pair will be placed on your public and secret key rings. You can later use the '-kx' command option to extract (copy) your new public key from your public key ring and place it in a separate public key file suitable for distribution to your friends. The public key file can be sent to your friends for inclusion in their public key rings. Naturally, you keep your secret key file to yourself, and you should include it on your secret key ring. Each secret key on a key ring is individually protected with its own pass phrase.

Never give your secret key to anyone else. For the same reason, don't make key pairs for your friends. Everyone should make their own key pair. Always keep physical control of your secret key, and don't risk exposing it by storing it on a remote timesharing computer. Keep it on your own personal computer.

If PGP complains about not being able to find the *PGP User's Guide* on your computer and refuses to generate a key pair without it, don't panic. Just read the explanation of the NOMANUAL parameter in chapter 9.

Adding a Key to Your Key Ring

Sometimes you will want to add to your keyring a key provided to you by someone else, in the form of a keyfile.

To add a public or secret key file's contents to your public or secret key ring (note that '[brackets]' denote an optional field):

```
pgp -ka keyfile [keyring]
```

The *keyfile* extension defaults to '.pgp'. The optional keyring file name defaults to 'pubring.pgp' or 'secring.pgp', depending on whether the keyfile contains a public or a secret key. You may specify a different key ring file name, with the extension defaulting to '.pgp'.

If the key is already on your key ring, PGP will not add it again. All of the keys in the keyfile are added to the keyring, except for duplicates.

Later in the manual, we will explain the concept of certifying keys with signatures. If the key being added has attached signatures certifying it, the signatures are added with the key. If the key is already on your key ring, PGP just merges in any new certifying signatures for that key that you don't already have on your key ring.

PGP was originally designed to handle small personal keyrings. If you want to handle really big keyrings, see the section "Handling Large Public Keyrings" in chapter 8.

Removing a Key or User ID from Your Key Ring

To remove a key or a user ID from your public key ring, type:

```
pgp -kr userid [keyring]
```

This searches for the specified user ID in your key ring, and removes it if it finds a match. Remember that any fragment of the user ID will suffice for a match. The optional keyring file name is assumed to be literally 'pubring.pgp'. It can be omitted, or you can specify 'secring.pgp' if you want to remove a secret key. You may specify a different key ring file name. The default key ring extension is '.pgp'.

If more than one user ID exists for this key, you will be asked if you want to remove only the user ID you specified, while leaving the key and its other user IDs intact.

Extracting (Copying) a Key from Your Key Ring

To extract (copy) a key from your public or secret key ring, type:

pgp -kx *userid keyfile* [*keyring*]

This non-destructively copies the key specified by the user ID from your public or secret key ring to the specified key file. This is particularly useful if you want to give a copy of your public key to someone else.

If the key has any certifying signatures attached to it on your key ring, they are copied off along with the key.

If you want the extracted key represented in printable ASCII characters suitable for email purposes, use the '-kxa' options.

Viewing the Contents of Your Key Ring

To view the contents of your public key ring, type:

pgp -kv[v] [*userid*] [*keyring*]

This lists any keys in the key ring that match the specified user ID substring. If you omit the user ID, all of the keys in the key ring are listed. The optional keyring file name is assumed to be 'pubring.pgp'. It can be omitted, or you can specify 'secring.pgp' if you want to list secret keys. If you want to specify a different key ring file name, you can. The default key ring extension is '.pgp'.

Later in the manual, we will explain the concept of certifying keys with signatures. To see all the certifying signatures attached to each key, use the '-kvv' option:

pgp -kvv [*userid*] [*keyring*]

If you want to specify a particular key ring file name, but want to see all the keys in it, try this alternative approach:

pgp *keyfile*

With no command options specified, PGP lists all the keys in 'keyfile.pgp', and also attempts to add them to your key ring if they are not already on your key ring.

How to Protect Public Keys from Tampering

In a public key cryptosystem, you don't have to protect public keys from exposure. In fact, it's better if they are widely disseminated. But it is important to protect public keys from tampering, to make sure that a public key really belongs to whom it appears to belong to. This may be the most important vulnerability of a public-key cryptosystem. Let's first look at a potential disaster, then at how to safely avoid it with PGP.

Suppose you wanted to send a private message to Alice. You download Alice's public key certificate from an electronic bulletin board system (BBS). You encrypt your letter to Alice with this public key and send it to her through the BBS's email facility.

Unfortunately, unbeknownst to you or Alice, another user named Charlie has infiltrated the BBS and generated a public key of his own with Alice's user ID attached to it. He covertly substitutes his bogus key in place of Alice's real public key. You unwittingly use this bogus key belonging to Charlie instead of Alice's public key. All looks normal because this bogus key has Alice's user ID. Now Charlie can decipher the message intended for Alice because he has the matching secret key. He may even re-encrypt the deciphered message with Alice's real public key and send it on to her so that no one suspects any wrongdoing. Furthermore, he can even make apparently good signatures from Alice with this secret key because everyone will use the bogus public key to check Alice's signatures.

The only way to prevent this disaster is to prevent anyone from tampering with public keys. If you got Alice's public key directly from Alice, this is no problem. But that may be difficult if Alice is a thousand miles away, or is currently unreachable.

Perhaps you could get Alice's public key from a mutual trusted friend David who knows he has a good copy of Alice's public key. David could sign Alice's public key, vouching for the integrity of Alice's public key. David would create this signature with his own secret key.

This would create a signed public key certificate, and would show that Alice's key had not been tampered with. This requires you have a known good copy of David's public key to check his signature. Perhaps David could provide Alice with a signed copy of your public key also. David is thus serving as an "introducer" between you and Alice.

This signed public key certificate for Alice could be uploaded by David or Alice to the BBS, and you could download it later. You could then check the signature via David's public key and thus be assured that this is really Alice's public key. No impostor can fool you into accepting his own bogus key as Alice's because no one else can forge signatures made by David.

A widely trusted person could even specialize in providing this service of "introducing" users to each other by providing signatures for their public key certificates. This trusted person could be regarded as a "key server", or as a "Certifying Authority". Any public key certificates bearing the key server's signature could be trusted as truly belonging to whom they appear to belong to. All users who wanted to participate would need a known good copy of just the key server's public key, so that the key server's signatures could be verified.

A trusted centralized key server or Certifying Authority is especially appropriate for large impersonal centrally-controlled corporate or government institutions. Some institutional environments use hierarchies of Certifying Authorities.

For more decentralized grassroots "guerrilla style" environments, allowing all users to act as a trusted introducers for their friends would probably work better than a centralized key server. PGP tends to emphasize this organic decentralized non-institutional approach. It better reflects the natural way humans interact on a personal social level, and allows people to better choose who they can trust for key management.

This whole business of protecting public keys from tampering is the single most difficult problem in practical public key applications. It is the Achilles' heel of public key cryptography, and a lot of software complexity is tied up in solving this one problem.

You should use a public key only after you are sure that it is a good public key that has not been tampered with, and actually belongs to the person it claims to. You can be sure of this if you got this public key certificate directly from its owner, or if it bears the signature of someone else that you trust, from whom you already have a good public key. Also, the user ID should have the full name of the key's owner, not just her first name.

No matter how tempted you are—and you will be tempted— never, *never* give in to expediency and trust a public key you downloaded from a bulletin board, unless it is signed by someone you trust. That uncertified public key could have been tampered with by anyone, maybe even by the system administrator of the bulletin board.

If you are asked to sign someone else's public key certificate, make certain that it really belongs to that person named in the user ID of that public key certificate. This is because your signature on her public key certificate is a promise by you that this public key really belongs to her. Other people who trust you will accept her public key because it bears your signature. It may be ill-advised to rely on hearsay—don't sign her public key unless you have independent firsthand knowledge that it really belongs to her. Preferably, you should sign it only if you got it directly from her.

In order to sign a public key, you must be far more certain of that key's ownership than if you merely want to use that key to encrypt a message. To be convinced of a key's validity enough to use it, certifying signatures from trusted introducers should suffice. But to sign a key yourself, you should require your own independent firsthand knowledge of who owns that key. Perhaps you could call the key's owner on the phone and read the key file to her to get her to confirm that the key you have really is her key—and make sure you really are talking to the right person. See the section "Verifying a Public Key over the Phone" in chapter 8 for further details.

Bear in mind that your signature on a public key certificate does not vouch for the integrity of that person, but only vouches for the integrity (the ownership) of that person's public key. You aren't risking your credibility by signing the public key of a sociopath, if you were completely confident that the key really belonged to him. Other people would accept that key as belonging to him because you signed it (assuming they trust you), but they wouldn't trust that key's owner. Trusting a key is not the same as trusting the key's owner.

Trust is not necessarily transferable; I have a friend who I trust not to lie. He's a gullible person who trusts the President not to lie. That doesn't mean I trust the President not to lie. This is just common sense. If I trust Alice's signature on a key, and Alice trusts Charlie's signature on a key, that does not imply that I have to trust Charlie's signature on a key.

It would be a good idea to keep your own public key on hand with a collection of certifying signatures attached from a variety of "introducers", in the hopes that most people will trust at least one of the introducers who vouch for your own public key's validity. You could post your key with its attached collection of certifying signatures on various electronic bulletin boards. If you sign someone else's public key, return it to them with your signature so that they can add it to their own collection of credentials for their own public key.

PGP keeps track of which keys on your public key ring are properly certified with signatures from introducers that you trust. All you have to do is tell PGP which people you trust as introducers, and certify their keys yourself with your own ultimately trusted key. PGP can take it from there, automatically validating any other keys that have been signed by your designated introducers. And of course you may directly sign more keys yourself. More on this later.

Make sure no one else can tamper with your own public key ring. Checking a new signed public key certificate must ultimately depend on the integrity of the trusted public keys that are already on your own public key ring. Maintain physical control of your public key ring, preferably on your own personal computer rather than on a remote timesharing system, just as you would do for your secret key. This is to protect it from tampering, not from disclosure. Keep a trusted backup copy of your public key ring and your secret key ring on write-protected media.

Since your own trusted public key is used as a final authority to directly or indirectly certify all the other keys on your key ring, it is the most important key to protect from tampering. To detect any tampering of your own ultimately-trusted public key, PGP can be set up to automatically compare your public key against a backup copy on write-protected media. For details, see the description of the '-kc' key ring check command in the section "Checking If Everything Is OK on Your Public Key Ring" in chapter 8.

PGP generally assumes you will maintain physical security over your system and your key rings, as well as your copy of PGP itself. If an intruder can tamper with your disk, then in theory he can tamper with PGP itself, rendering moot the safeguards PGP may have to detect tampering with keys.

One somewhat complicated way to protect your own whole public key ring from tampering is to sign the whole ring with your own secret key. You could do this by making a detached signature certificate of the public key ring, by signing the ring with the '-sb' options (see "Separating Signatures from Messages" in chapter 8). Unfortunately, you would still have to keep a separate trusted copy of your own public key around to check the signature you made. You couldn't rely on your own public key stored on your public key ring to check the signature you made for the whole ring, because that is part of what you're trying to check.

How Does PGP Keep Track of Which Keys Are Valid?

Before you read this section, be sure to read the previous section on protecting public keys from tampering.

PGP keeps track of which keys on your public key ring are properly certified with signatures from introducers that you trust. All you have to do is tell PGP which people you trust as introducers, and certify their keys yourself with your own ultimately trusted key. PGP can take it from there, automatically validating any other keys that have been signed by your designated introducers. And of course you may directly sign more keys yourself.

There are two entirely separate criteria PGP uses to judge a public key's usefulness. Don't get them confused:

1. Does the key actually belong to whom it appears to belong? In other words, has it been certified with a trusted signature?

2. Does it belong to someone you can trust to certify other keys?

PGP can calculate the answer to the first question. To answer the second question, PGP must be explicitly told by you, the user. When you supply the answer to question 2, PGP can then calculate the answer to question 1 for other keys signed by the introducer you designated as trusted.

Keys that have been certified by a trusted introducer are deemed valid by PGP. The keys belonging to trusted introducers must themselves be certified either by you or by other trusted introducers.

PGP also allows for the possibility of you having several shades of trust for people to act as introducers. Your trust for a key's owner to act as an introducer does not just reflect your estimation of their personal integrity. It should also reflect how competent you think they are at understanding key management and using good judgment in signing keys. You can designate a person to PGP as unknown, untrusted, marginally trusted, or completely trusted to certify other public keys. This trust information is stored on your key ring with their key, but when you tell PGP to copy a key off your key ring, PGP will not copy the trust information along with the key, because your private opinions on trust are regarded as confidential.

When PGP is calculating the validity of a public key, it examines the trust level of all the attached certifying signatures. It computes a weighted score of validity—two marginally trusted signatures are deemed as credible as one fully trusted signature. PGP's skepticism is adjustable. For example, you may tune PGP to require two fully trusted signatures or three marginally trusted signatures to judge a key as valid.

Your own key is "axiomatically" valid to PGP, needing no introducer's signature to prove its validity. PGP knows which public keys are yours, by looking for the corresponding secret keys on the secret key ring. PGP also assumes you ultimately trust yourself to certify other keys.

As time goes on, you will accumulate keys from other people that you may want to designate as trusted introducers. Everyone else will each choose their own trusted introducers. And everyone will gradually accumulate and distribute with their key a collection of certifying signatures from other people, with the expectation that anyone receiving it will trust at least one or two of the signatures. This will cause the emergence of a decentralized fault-tolerant web of confidence for all public keys.

This unique grass-roots approach contrasts sharply with government standard public key management schemes, such as Internet Privacy Enhanced Mail (PEM), which are based on centralized control and mandatory centralized trust. The standard schemes rely on a hierarchy of Certifying Authorities who dictate who you must trust. PGP's decentralized probabilistic method for determining public key legitimacy is the centerpiece of its key management architecture. PGP lets you alone choose who you trust, putting you at the top of your own private certification pyramid. PGP is for people who prefer to pack their own parachutes.

How to Protect Secret Keys from Disclosure

Protect your own secret key and your pass phrase carefully. Really, *really* carefully. If your secret key is ever compromised, you'd better get the word out quickly to all interested parties (good luck) before someone else uses it to make signatures in your name. For example, they could use it to sign bogus public key certificates, which could create problems for many people, especially if your signature is widely trusted. And of course, a compromise of your own secret key could expose all messages sent to you.

To protect your secret key, you can start by always keeping physical control of your secret key. Keeping it on your personal computer at home is OK, or keep it in your notebook computer that you can carry with you. If you must use an office computer that you don't always have physical control of, then keep your public and secret key rings on a write-protected removable floppy disk, and don't leave it behind when you leave the office. It wouldn't be a good idea to allow your secret key to reside on a remote timesharing computer, such as a remote dial-in Unix system. Someone could eavesdrop on your modem line and capture your pass phrase, and then obtain your actual secret key from the remote system. You should only use your secret key on a machine that you have physical control over.

Don't store your pass phrase anywhere on the computer that has your secret key file. Storing both the secret key and the pass phrase on the same computer is as dangerous as keeping your PIN in the same wallet as your Automatic Teller Machine bank card. You don't want somebody to get their hands on your disk containing both the pass phrase and the secret key file. It would be most secure if you just memorize your pass phrase and don't store it anywhere but your brain. If you feel you must write down your pass phrase, keep it well protected, perhaps even more well protected than the secret key file.

And keep backup copies of your secret key ring—remember, you have the only copy of your secret key, and losing it will render useless all the copies of your public key that you have spread throughout the world.

The decentralized non-institutional approach PGP uses to manage public keys has its benefits, but unfortunately this also means we can't rely on a single centralized list of which keys have been compromised. This makes it a bit harder to contain the damage of a secret key compromise. You just have to spread the word and hope everyone hears about it.

If the worst case happens—your secret key and pass phrase are both compromised (hopefully you will find this out somehow)—you will have to issue a *key compromise* certificate. This kind of certificate is used to warn other people to stop using your public key. You can use PGP to create such a certificate by using the '-kd' command. Then you must somehow send this compromise certificate to everyone else on the planet, or at least to all your friends and their friends, et cetera. Their own PGP software will install this key compromise certificate on their public key rings and will automatically prevent them from accidentally using your public key ever again. You can then generate a new secret/public key pair and publish the new public key. You could send out one package containing both your new public key and the key compromise certificate for your old key.

Revoking a Public Key

Suppose your secret key and your pass phrase are somehow both compromised. You have to get the word out to the rest of the world, so that they will all stop using your public key. To do this, you will have to issue a "key compromise", or "key revocation" certificate to revoke your public key.

To generate a certificate to revoke your own key, use the '-kd' command:

```
pgp -kd your_userid
```

This certificate bears your signature, made with the same key you are revoking. You should widely disseminate this key revocation certificate as soon as possible. Other people who receive it can add it to their public key rings, and their PGP software then automatically prevents them from accidentally using your old public key ever again. You can then generate a new secret/public key pair and publish the new public key.

You may choose to revoke your key for some other reason than the compromise of a secret key. If so, you may still use the same mechanism to revoke it.

What If You Lose Your Secret Key?

Normally, if you want to revoke your own secret key, you can use the '-kd' command to issue a revocation certificate, signed with your own secret key, as described in the previous section.

But what can you do if you lose your secret key, or if your secret key is destroyed? You can't revoke it yourself, because you must use your own secret key to revoke it, and you don't have it anymore. A future version of PGP will offer a more secure means of revoking keys in these circumstances, allowing trusted introducers to certify that a public key has been revoked. But for now, you will have to get the word out through whatever informal means you can, asking users to "disable" your public key on their own individual public key rings.

Other users may disable your public key on their own public key rings by using the '-kd' command. If a user ID is specified that does not correspond to a secret key on the secret key ring, the '-kd' command will look for that user ID on the public key ring, and mark that public key as disabled. A disabled key may not be used to encrypt any messages, and may not be extracted from the key ring with the '-kx' command. It can still be used to check signatures, but a warning is displayed. And if the user tries to add the same key again to his key ring, it will not work because the disabled key is already on the key ring. These combined features will help curtail the further spread of a disabled key.

If the specified public key is already disabled, the '-kd' command will ask if you want the key reenabled.

6

Advanced Topics

Most of the truly advanced topics are covered in Part II, but here are a few more detailed topics that bear mentioning here.

Sending Ciphertext through Email Channels

Many electronic mail systems only allow messages made of ASCII text, not the 8-bit raw binary data that ciphertext is made of. To get around this problem, PGP supports ASCII radix-64 format for ciphertext messages, similar to the Internet Privacy Enhanced Mail (PEM) format, as well as the Internet MIME format. This special format represents binary data by using only printable ASCII characters, so it is useful for transmitting binary encrypted data through 7-bit channels or for sending binary encrypted data as normal email text. This format acts as a form of *transport armor*, protecting it against corruption as it travels through intersystem gateways on Internet. PGP also appends a CRC to detect transmission errors.

Radix-64 format converts the plaintext by expanding groups of 3 binary 8-bit bytes into 4 printable ASCII characters, so the file grows by about 33%. But this expansion isn't so bad when you consider that the file probably was compressed more than that by PGP before it was encrypted.

To produce a ciphertext file in ASCII radix-64 format, just add the 'a' option when encrypting or signing a message, like so:

```
pgp -esa message .txt her_userid
```

This example produces a ciphertext file called '*message*.asc' that contains data in a MIME-like ASCII radix-64 format. This file can be easily uploaded into a text editor through 7-bit channels for transmission as normal email on the Internet or any other email network.

Decrypting the radix-64 transport-armored message is no different than a normal decrypt. For example:

pgp *message*

PGP automatically looks for the ASCII file '*message*.asc' before it looks for the binary file '*message*.pgp'. It recognizes that the file is in radix-64 format and converts it back to binary before processing as it normally does, producing as a by-product a '.pgp' ciphertext file in binary form. The final output file is in normal plaintext form, just as it was in the original file '*message*.txt'.

Most Internet email facilities prohibit sending messages that are more than 50,000 or 65,000 bytes long. Longer messages must be broken into smaller chunks that can be mailed separately. If your encrypted message is very large, and you requested radix-64 format, PGP automatically breaks it up into chunks that are each small enough to send via email. The chunks are put into files named with extensions 'as1', 'as2', 'as3', etc. The recipient must concatenate these separate files back together in their proper order into one big file before decrypting it. While decrypting, PGP ignores any extraneous text in mail headers that are not enclosed in the radix-64 message blocks.

If you want to send a public key to someone else in radix-64 format, just add the '-a' option while extracting the key from your keyring.

If you forgot to use the '-a' option when you made a ciphertext file or extracted a key, you may still directly convert the binary file into radix-64 format by simply using the '-a' option alone, without any encryption specified. PGP converts it to a '-.asc' file.

If you sign a plaintext file without encrypting it, PGP will normally compress it after signing it, rendering it unreadable to the casual human observer. This is a suitable way of storing signed files in archival applications. But if you want to send the signed message as email, and the the original plaintext message is in text (not binary) form, there is a way to send it through an email channel in such a way that the plaintext does not get compressed, and the ASCII armor is applied only to the binary signature certificate, but not to the plaintext message. This makes it possible for the recipient to read the signed message with human eyes, without the aid of PGP. Of course, PGP is still needed to actually check the signature. For further information on this feature, see the explanation of the CLEARSIG parameter in chapter 9.

Sometimes you may want to send a binary data file through an email channel without encrypting or signing it with PGP. Some people use the Unix uuencode utility for that purpose. PGP can also be used for that purpose, by simply using the '-a' option alone, and it does a better job than the uuencode utility. For further details, see the section "Using PGP as a Better Uuencode" in chapter 8.

Environmental Variable for Path Name

PGP uses several special files for its purposes, such as your standard key ring files 'pubring.pgp' or 'secring.pgp', the random number seed file 'randseed.bin', the PGP configuration file 'config.txt' (or 'pgp.ini', or '.pgprc'), and the foreign language string translation file 'language.txt'. These special files can be kept in any directory, by setting the environmental variable PGPPATH to the desired pathname. For example, on MSDOS, you can use the following shell command:

```
SET PGPPATH=C:\PGP
```

This command makes PGP assume that your public key ring filename is 'C:\PGP\pubring.pgp'. Assuming, of course, that this directory exists. Use your favorite text editor to modify your MSDOS 'AUTOEXEC.BAT' file to automatically set up this variable whenever you start up your system. If PGPPATH remains undefined, these special files are assumed to be in the current directory.

Setting Parameters in the PGP Configuration File

PGP has a number of user-settable parameters that can be defined in a special PGP configuration text file called 'config.txt', in the directory pointed to by the shell environmental variable PGPPATH. Having a configuration file enables the user to define various flags and parameters for PGP without the burden of having to always define these parameters in the PGP command line.

In the interest of complying with local operating system file naming conventions, for Unix systems this configuration file may also be named '.pgprc', and on MSDOS systems it may also be named 'pgp.ini'.

With these configuration parameters, for example, you can control where PGP stores its temporary scratch files, or you can select what foreign language PGP will use to display its diagnostics messages and user prompts, or you can adjust PGP's level of skepticism in determining a key's validity based on the number of certifying signatures it has.

For more details on setting these configuration parameters, see chapter 9.

Vulnerabilities, in Brief

No data security system is impenetrable. PGP can be circumvented in a variety of ways. Potential vulnerabilities you should be aware of include compromising your pass phrase or secret key, public key tampering, files that you deleted but are still somewhere on the disk, viruses and Trojan horses, breaches in your physical security, electromagnetic emissions, exposure on multi-user systems, traffic analysis, and perhaps even direct cryptanalysis.

For a detailed discussion of these issues, see chapter 11.

7

Beware of Snake Oil

When examining a cryptographic software package, the question always remains, why should you trust this product? Even if you examined the source code yourself, not everyone has the cryptographic experience to judge the security. Even if you are an experienced cryptographer, subtle weaknesses in the algorithms could still elude you.

When I was in college in the early seventies, I devised what I believed was a brilliant encryption scheme. A simple pseudorandom number stream was added to the plaintext stream to create ciphertext. This would seemingly thwart any frequency analysis of the ciphertext, and would be uncrackable even to the most resourceful government intelligence agencies. I felt so smug about my achievement. So cock-sure.

Years later, I discovered this same scheme in several introductory cryptography texts and tutorial papers. How nice. Other cryptographers had thought of the same scheme. Unfortunately, the scheme was presented as a simple homework assignment on how to use elementary cryptanalytic techniques to trivially crack it. So much for my brilliant scheme.

From this humbling experience I learned how easy it is to fall into a false sense of security when devising an encryption algorithm. Most people don't realize how fiendishly difficult it is to devise an encryption algorithm that can withstand a prolonged and determined attack by a resourceful opponent. Many mainstream software engineers have developed equally naive encryption schemes (often even the very same encryption scheme), and some of them have been incorporated into commercial encryption software packages and sold for good money to thousands of unsuspecting users.

This is like selling automotive seat belts that look good and feel good, but snap open in even the slowest crash test. Depending on them may be worse than not wearing seat belts at all. No one suspects they are bad until a real crash. Depending on weak cryptographic software may cause you to unknowingly place sensitive information at risk. You might not otherwise have done so if you had no cryptographic software at all. Perhaps you may never even discover your data has been compromised.

Sometimes commercial packages use the Federal Data Encryption Standard (DES), a fairly good conventional algorithm recommended by the government for commercial use (but not for classified information, oddly enough—hmmm). There are several "modes of operation" the DES can use, some of them better than others. The government specifically recommends not using the weakest simplest mode for messages, the Electronic Codebook (ECB) mode. But they do recommend the stronger and more complex Cipher Feedback (CFB) or Cipher Block Chaining (CBC) modes.

Unfortunately, most of the commercial encryption packages I've looked at use ECB mode. When I've talked to the authors of a number of these implementations, they say they've never heard of CBC or CFB modes, and didn't know anything about the weaknesses of ECB mode. The very fact that they haven't even learned enough cryptography to know these elementary concepts is not reassuring. And they sometimes manage their DES keys in inappropriate or insecure ways. Also, these same software packages often include a second faster encryption algorithm that can be used instead of the slower DES. The author of the package often thinks his proprietary faster algorithm is as secure as the DES, but after questioning him I usually discover that it's just a variation of my own brilliant scheme from college days. Or maybe he won't even reveal how his proprietary encryption scheme works, but assures me it's a brilliant scheme and I should trust it. I'm sure he believes that his algorithm is brilliant, but how can I know that without seeing it?

In all fairness I must point out that in most cases these terribly weak products do not come from companies that specialize in cryptographic technology.

Even the really good software packages, that use the DES in the correct modes of operation, still have problems. Standard DES uses a 56-bit key, which is too small by today's standards, and may now be easily broken by exhaustive key searches on special high-speed machines. The DES has reached the end of its useful life, and so has any software package that relies on it.

There is a company called AccessData (87 East 600 South, Orem, Utah 84058, phone 1-800-658-5199) that sells a package for $185 that cracks the built-in encryption schemes used by WordPerfect, Lotus 1-2-3, MS Excel, Symphony, Quattro Pro, Paradox, and MS Word 2.0. It doesn't simply guess passwords—it does real cryptanalysis. Some people buy it when they forget their password for their own files. Law enforcement agencies buy it too, so they can read files they seize. I talked to Eric Thompson, the author, and he said his program only takes a split second to crack them, but he put in some delay loops to slow it down so it doesn't look so easy to the customer. He also told me that the password encryption feature of 'PKZIP' files can often be easily broken, and that his law enforcement customers already have that service regularly provided to them from another vendor.

In some ways, cryptography is like pharmaceuticals. Its integrity may be absolutely crucial. Bad penicillin looks the same as good penicillin. You can tell if your spreadsheet software is wrong, but how do you tell if your cryptography package is weak? The ciphertext produced by a weak encryption algorithm looks as good as ciphertext produced by a strong encryption algorithm. There's a lot of snake oil out there. A lot of quack cures. Unlike the patent medicine hucksters of old, these software implementors usually don't even know their stuff is snake oil. They may be good software engineers, but they usually haven't even read any of the academic literature in cryptography. But they think they can write good cryptographic software. And why not? After all, it seems intuitively easy to do so. And their software seems to work okay.

Anyone who thinks they have devised an unbreakable encryption scheme either is an incredibly rare genius or is naive and inexperienced. Unfortunately, I sometimes have to deal with would-be cryptographers who want to make "improvements" to PGP by adding encryption algorithms of their own design.

I remember a conversation with Brian Snow, a highly placed senior cryptographer with the NSA. He said he would never trust an encryption algorithm designed by someone who had not "earned their bones" by first spending a lot of time cracking codes. That did make a lot of sense. I observed that practically no one in the commercial world of cryptography qualified under this criterion. "Yes," he said with a self assured smile. "And that makes our job at NSA so much easier." A chilling thought. I didn't qualify either.

The government has peddled snake oil too. After World War II, the United States sold German Enigma ciphering machines to third world governments. But they didn't tell them that the Allies cracked the Enigma code during the war, a fact that remained classified for many years. Even today many Unix systems worldwide use the Enigma cipher for file encryption, in part because the government has created legal obstacles against using better algorithms. They even tried to prevent the initial publication of the RSA algorithm in 1977. And they have squashed essentially all commercial efforts to develop effective secure telephones for the general public.

The principal job of the U.S. government's National Security Agency is to gather intelligence, principally by covertly tapping into people's private communications (see James Bamford's book, *The Puzzle Palace*). The NSA has amassed considerable skill and resources for cracking codes. When people can't get good cryptography to protect themselves, it makes NSA's job much easier. NSA also has the responsibility of approving and recommending encryption algorithms. Some critics charge that this is a conflict of interest, like putting the fox in charge of guarding the hen house. NSA has been pushing a conventional encryption algorithm that they designed, and they won't tell anybody how it works because that's classified. They want others to trust it and use it. But any cryptographer can tell you that a well-designed encryption algorithm does not have to be classified to remain secure. Only the keys should need protection. How does anyone else really know if NSA's classified algorithm is secure? It's not that hard for NSA to design an encryption algorithm that only they can crack, if no one else can review the algorithm. Are they deliberately selling snake oil?

There are three main factors that have undermined the quality of commercial cryptographic software in the United States. The first is the virtually universal lack of competence of implementors of commercial encryption software (although this is starting to change since the publication of PGP). Every software engineer fancies himself a cryptographer, which has led to the proliferation of really bad crypto software. The second is the NSA deliberately and systematically suppressing all the good commercial encryption technology, by legal intimidation and economic pressure. Part of this pressure is brought to bear by stringent export controls on encryption software which, by the economics of software marketing, has the net effect of suppressing domestic encryption software. The other principal method of suppression comes from the granting all the software patents for all the public key encryption algorithms to a single company, affording a single choke point to suppress the spread of this technology. The net effect of all this is that before PGP was published, there was almost no highly secure general purpose encryption software available in the United States.

I'm not as certain about the security of PGP as I once was about my brilliant encryption software from college. If I were, that would be a bad sign. But I'm pretty sure that PGP does not contain any glaring weaknesses (although it may contain bugs). The crypto algorithms were developed by people at high levels of civilian cryptographic academia, and have been individually subject to extensive peer review. Source code is available to facilitate peer review of PGP and to help dispel the fears of some users. It's reasonably well researched, and has been years in the making. And I don't work for the NSA. I hope it doesn't require too large a "leap of faith" to trust the security of PGP.

II

Special Topics

8
Useful Details

Part II covers advanced topics and is optional for most readers, except for chapter 12 on legal issues, which everyone should read.

Selecting Keys via Key ID

In all commands that let the user type a user ID or fragment of a user ID to select a key, the hexadecimal key ID may be used instead. Just use the key ID, with a prefix of '0x', in place of the user ID. For example:

```
pgp -kv 0x67F7
```

This would display all keys that had '67F7' as part of their key IDs.

This feature is particularly useful if you have two different keys from the same person, with the same user ID. You can unambiguously pick which key you want by specifying the key ID.

Separating Signatures from Messages

Normally, signature certificates are physically attached to the text they sign. This makes it convenient in simple cases to check signatures. It is desirable in some circumstances to have signature certificates stored separately from the messages they sign. It is possible to generate signature certificates that are detached from the text they sign. To do this, combine the '-b' (break) option with the '-s' (sign) option. For example:

```
pgp -sb letter.txt
```

This example produces an isolated signature certificate in a file called *letter.sig*. The contents of *letter.txt* are not appended to the signature certificate.

After creating the signature certificate file (*letter.sig* in the above example), send it along with the original text file to the recipient. The recipient must have both files to check the signature integrity. When the recipient attempts to process the signature file, PGP notices that there is no text in the same file with the signature and prompts the user for the filename of the text. Only then can PGP properly check the signature integrity. If the recipient knows in advance that the signature is detached from the text file, she can specify both filenames on the command line:

```
pgp letter.sig letter.txt
```

or:

```
pgp letter letter.txt
```

PGP will not have to prompt for the text file name in this case.

A detached signature certificate is useful if you want to keep the signature certificate in a separate certificate log. A detached signature of an executable program is also useful for detecting a subsequent virus infection. It is also useful if more than one party must sign a document such as a legal contract, without nesting signatures. Each person's signature is independent.

If you receive a ciphertext file that has the signature certificate glued to the message, you can still pry the signature certificate away from the message during the decryption. You can do this with the '-b' option during decrypt, like so:

```
pgp -b letter
```

This decrypts the *letter.pgp* file and if there is a signature in it, PGP checks the signature and detaches it from the rest of the message, storing it in the file *letter.sig*.

Decrypting the Message and Leaving the Signature on It

Usually, you want PGP to completely unravel a ciphertext file, decrypting it and checking the nested signature if there is one, peeling away the layers until you are left with only the original plaintext file.

But sometimes you want to decrypt an encrypted file, and leave the inner signature still attached, so that you are left with a decrypted signed message. This may be useful if you want to send a copy of a signed document to a third party, perhaps re-enciphering it. For example, suppose you get a message signed by Charlie, encrypted to you. You want to decrypt it, and, leaving Charlie's signature on it, you want to send it to Alice, perhaps re-enciphering it with Alice's public key. No problem. PGP can handle that.

To simply decrypt a message and leave the signature on it intact, type:

```
pgp -d letter
```

This decrypts *letter.pgp*, and if there is an inner signature, it is left intact with the decrypted plaintext in the output file.

Now you can archive it, or maybe re-encrypt it and send it to someone else.

Sending ASCII Text Files across Different Machine Environments

You may use PGP to encrypt any kind of plaintext file, binary 8-bit data or ASCII text. Probably the most common usage of PGP will be for email, when the plaintext is ASCII text.

ASCII text is sometimes represented differently on different machines. For example, on an MSDOS system, all lines of ASCII text are terminated with a carriage return followed by a linefeed. On a Unix system, all lines end with just a linefeed. On a Macintosh, all lines end with just a carriage return. This is a sad fact of life.

Normal unencrypted ASCII text messages are often automatically translated to some common canonical form when they are transmitted from one machine to another. *Canonical* text has a carriage return and a linefeed at the end of each line of text. For example, the popular Kermit communication protocol can convert text to canonical form when transmitting it to another system. This gets converted back to local text line terminators by the receiving Kermit. This makes it easy to share text files across different systems.

But encrypted text cannot be automatically converted by a communication protocol, because the plaintext is hidden by encipherment. To remedy this inconvenience, PGP lets you specify that the plaintext should be treated as ASCII text (not binary data) and should be converted to canonical text form before it gets encrypted. At the receiving end, the decrypted plaintext is automatically converted back to whatever text form is appropriate for the local environment.

To make PGP assume the plaintext is text that should be converted to canonical text before encryption, just add the '-t' option when encrypting or signing a message, like so:

```
pgp -et message.txt her_userid
```

This mode is automatically turned off if PGP detects that the plaintext file contains what it thinks is non-text binary data.

If you need to use the '-t' option a lot, you can just turn on the TEXTMODE flag in the PGP configuration file. That's what I do.

For PGP users that use non-English 8-bit character sets, when PGP converts text to canonical form, it may convert data from the local character set into the LATIN1 (ISO 8859-1 Latin Alphabet 1) character set, depending on the setting of the CHARSET parameter in the PGP configuration file. LATIN1 is a superset of ASCII, with extra characters added for many European languages.

Using PGP as a Better Uuencode

A lot of people in the Unix world send binary data files through email channels by using the Unix uuencode utility to convert the file into printable ASCII characters that can be sent via email. No encryption is involved, so neither the sender nor the recipient need any special keys. The uuencode format was designed for a similar purpose as PGP's radix-64 ASCII transport armor format described in chapter 6, but not as good. A different radix-64 character set is used. uuencode has its problems, such as (1) several slightly incompatible character sets for different versions of uuencode in the MSDOS and Unix worlds, and (2) the data can be corrupted by some email gateways that strip trailing blanks or do other modifications to the character set used by uuencode.

PGP may be used in a manner that offers the same general features as uuencode, and then some. You can get PGP to just convert a file into PGP's radix-64 ASCII transport armor format, but you don't have to encrypt the file or sign it, so no keys are needed by either party. Simply use the '-a' option alone. For example:

pgp -a *filename*

This would produce a radix-64 armored file called 'filename.asc'.

If you read the section "Sending Ciphertext through Email Channels" in chapter 6, you will see that PGP's approach offers several important advantages over the uuencode approach:

- PGP will break big files up into chunks small enough to email.
- PGP will append a CRC error detection code to each chunk.
- PGP will attempt to compress the data before converting it to radix-64 armor.
- PGP's radix-64 character set is more resilient to email character conversions than the one used by uuencode.
- Textfiles can be converted by the sender to canonical text format, as explained in the last section.

The recipient can restore the sender's original filename by unwrapping the message with PGP's '-p' option. You can use pgp -a in any situation in which you could have used uuencode, if the recipient also has PGP.

Leaving No Traces of Plaintext on the Disk

After PGP makes a ciphertext file for you, you can have PGP automatically overwrite the plaintext file and delete it, leaving no trace of plaintext on the disk so that no one can recover it later using a disk block scanning utility. This is useful if the plaintext file contains sensitive information that you don't want to keep around.

To wipe out the plaintext file after producing the ciphertext file, just add the '-w' (wipe) option when encrypting or signing a message, like so:

pgp -esw *message.txt her_userid*

This example creates the ciphertext file 'message.pgp', and the plaintext file 'message.txt' is destroyed beyond recovery.

Obviously, you should be careful with this option. Also note that this will not wipe out any fragments of plaintext that your word processor might have created on the disk while you were editing the message before running PGP. Most word processors create backup files, scratch files, or both. Also, it overwrites the file only once, which is enough to thwart conventional disk recovery efforts, but not enough to withstand a determined and sophisticated effort to recover the faint magnetic traces of the data using special disk recovery hardware.

Displaying Decrypted Plaintext on Your Screen

To view the decrypted plaintext output on your screen (like the Unix-style more command), without writing it to a file, use the '-m' (more) option while decrypting:

pgp -m *ciphertextfile*

This displays the decrypted plaintext display on your screen one screenful at a time.

Making a Message for Her Eyes Only

To specify that the recipient's decrypted plaintext will be shown *only* on her screen and will not be saved to disk, add the '-m' option:

pgp -sem *message.txt her_userid*

Later, when the recipient decrypts the ciphertext with her secret
key and pass phrase, the plaintext will be displayed on her screen
but will not be saved to disk. The text will be displayed as it would
if she used the Unix `more` command, one screenful at a time. If
she wants to read the message again, she will have to decrypt the
ciphertext again.

This feature is the safest way for you to prevent your sensitive
message from being inadvertently left on the recipient's disk. This
feature was added at the request of a user who wanted to send
intimate messages to his lover, but was afraid she might accidentally
leave the decrypted messages on her husband's computer.

Note that this feature will not prevent a clever and determined
person from finding a way to save the decrypted plaintext to disk.
It will, however, help prevent a casual user from doing so inadvertently.

Preserving the Original Plaintext Filename

Normally, PGP names the decrypted plaintext output file with a
name similar to the input ciphertext filename, but dropping the
extension. Or, you can override that convention by specifying an
output plaintext filename on the command line with the '`-o`'
option. For most email, this is a reasonable way to name the
plaintext file, because you get to decide its name when you decipher it, and your typical email messages often come from useless
original plaintext filenames like '`to_phil.txt`'.

But when PGP encrypts a plaintext file, it always saves the original
filename and attaches it to the plaintext before it compresses and
encrypts the plaintext. Normally, this hidden original filename is
discarded by PGP when it decrypts, but you can tell PGP you want
to preserve the original plaintext filename and use it as the name
of the decrypted plaintext output file. This is useful if PGP is used
on files whose names are important to preserve.

To recover the original plaintext filename while decrypting, add
the '`-p`' option, like so:

```
pgp -p ciphertextfile
```

I usually don't use this option, because if I did, about half of my incoming email would decrypt to the same plaintext filenames of 'to_phil.txt' or 'prz.txt'.

Editing Your User ID or Pass Phrase

Sometimes you may need to change your pass phrase, perhaps because someone looked over your shoulder while you typed it in.

Or you may need to change your user ID, because you got married and changed your name, or maybe you changed your email address. Or maybe you want to add a second or third user ID to your key, because you may be known by more than one name or email address or job title. PGP lets you attach more than one user ID to your key, any one of which may be used to look up your key on the key ring.

To edit your own userid or pass phrase for your secret key, type:

```
pgp -ke userid [keyring]
```

PGP prompts you for a new user ID or a new pass phrase.

If you edit your user ID, PGP actually adds a new user ID, without deleting the old one. If you want to delete an old user ID, you will have to do that in a separate operation.

The optional '[keyring]' parameter, if specified, must be a public keyring, not a secret keyring. The userid field must be your own userid, which PGP knows is yours because it appears on both your public keyring and your secret keyring. Both keyrings will be updated, even though you only specified the public keyring.

The '-ke' command works differently depending on whether you use it on a public or secret key. It can also be used to edit the trust parameters for a public key.

Editing the Trust Parameters for a Public Key

Sometimes you need to alter the trust parameters for a public key on your public key ring. For a discussion on what these trust parameters mean, see the section "How Does PGP Keep Track of Which Keys Are Valid?" in chapter 5.

To edit the trust parameters for a public key, type:

`pgp -ke` *userid* [*keyring*]

The optional '[*keyring*]' parameter, if specified, must be a public keyring, not a secret keyring.

Checking That Everything Is OK on Your Public Key Ring

Normally, PGP automatically checks any new keys or signatures on your public key ring and updates all the trust parameters and validity scores. In theory, it keeps all the key validity status information up to date as material is added to or deleted from your public key ring. But perhaps you may want to explicitly force PGP to perform a comprehensive analysis of your public key ring, checking all the certifying signatures, checking the trust parameters, updating all the validity scores, and checking your own ultimately-trusted key against a backup copy on a write-protected floppy disk. It may be a good idea to do this hygienic maintenance periodically to make sure nothing is wrong with your public key ring. To force PGP to perform a full analysis of your public key ring, use the '-kc' (key ring check) command:

`pgp -kc`

You can also make PGP check all the signatures for just a single selected public key by:

`pgp -kc` *userid* [*keyring*]

For further information on how the backup copy of your own key is checked, see the description of the BAKRING parameter in chapter 9.

Verifying a Public Key over the Phone

If you get a public key from someone that is not certified by anyone you trust, how can you tell if it's really their key? The best way to verify an uncertified key is to verify it over some independent channel other than the one you received the key through. One convenient way to tell, if you know this person and would recognize them on the phone, is to call them and verify their key over the telephone. Rather than reading their whole tiresome (ASCII-armored) key to them over the phone, you can just read their key's "fingerprint" to them. To see this fingerprint, use the '-kvc' command:

pgp -kvc *userid* [*keyring*]

This will display the key with the 16-byte digest of the public key components. Read this 16-byte fingerprint to the key's owner on the phone, while she checks it against her own, using the same '-kvc' command at her end.

You can both verify each other's keys this way, and then you can sign each other's keys with confidence. This is a safe and convenient way to get the key trust network started for your circle of friends.

Note that sending a key fingerprint via email is not the best way to verify the key, because email can be intercepted and modified. It's best to use a different channel than the one that was used to send the key itself. A good combination is to send the key via email, and the key fingerprint via a voice telephone conversation. Some people distribute their key fingerprint on their business cards, which looks really cool.

For current versions of PGP, the key fingerprint is computed using the MD5 hash function. A future version of PGP will optionally use a new and different hash function, SHA, instead of MD5.

If you don't know me, please don't call me to verify my key over the phone—I get too many calls like that. Since every PGP user has a copy of my public key, no one could tamper with all the copies that are out there. The discrepancy would soon be noticed by someone who checked it from more than one source, and word would soon get out on the Internet.

For those of you who want to verify my public key (included in the standard PGP release package), here are the particulars:

UserID: "Philip R. Zimmermann <prz@acm.org>"

```
Key Size: 1024 bits; Creation date: 21 May 1993;
KeyID: C7A966DD

Key fingerprint: 9E 94 45 13 39 83 5F 70
                 7B E7 D8 ED C4 BE 5A A6
```

The information printed above conceivably could still be tampered with in the electronic distribution of the *Official PGP User's Guide*. But if you read this in the printed version of the manual, available in bookstores from MIT Press, it's a safe bet that it really is my own key's fingerprint.

Handling Large Public Keyrings

PGP was originally designed for handling small personal keyrings for keeping all your friends on, like a personal rolodex. A couple hundred keys is a reasonable size for such a keyring. But as PGP has become more popular, people are now trying to add other large keyrings to their own keyring. Sometimes this involves adding thousands of keys to your keyring. PGP, in its present form, cannot perform this operation in a reasonable period of time, while you wait at your keyboard. Not for huge keyrings.

You may want to add a huge "imported" keyring to your own keyring, because you are only interested in a few dozen keys on the bigger keyring you are bringing in. If that's all you want from the other keyring, it would be more efficient if you extract the few keys you need from the big foreign keyring, and then add just these few keys to your own keyring. Use the '-kx' command to extract them from the foreign keyring, specifying the keyring name on the command line. Then add these extracted keys to your own keyring.

The real solution is to improve PGP to use advanced database techniques to manage large keyrings efficiently. We are working on this, and should have it done Real Soon Now. Until this happens, you will just have to use smaller keyrings, or be patient.

Using PGP as a Unix-Style Filter

Unix fans are accustomed to using Unix "pipes" to make two applications work together. The output of one application can be directly fed through a pipe to be read as input to another application. For this to work, the applications must be capable of reading the raw material from "standard input" and writing the finished output to "standard output". PGP can operate in this mode. If you don't understand what this means, then you probably don't need this feature.

To use a Unix-style filter mode, reading from standard input and writing to standard output, add the '-f' option, like so:

```
pgp -feast her_userid < inputfile > outputfile
```

This feature makes it easier to make PGP work with electronic mail applications.

When using PGP in filter mode to decrypt a ciphertext file, you may find it useful to use the PGPPASS environmental variable to hold the pass phrase, so that you won't be prompted for it. The PGPPASS feature is explained below.

Suppressing Unnecessary Questions: BATCHMODE

With the BATCHMODE flag enabled on the command line, PGP will not ask any unnecessary questions or prompt for alternate filenames. Here is an example of how to set this flag:

```
pgp +batchmode cipherfile
```

This is useful for running PGP non-interactively from Unix shell scripts or MSDOS batch files. Some key management commands still need user interaction even when BATCHMODE is on, so shell scripts may need to avoid them.

BATCHMODE may also be enabled to check the validity of a signature on a file. If there was no signature on the file, the exit code is 1. If it had a signature that was good, the exit code is 0.

Force Yes Answer to Confirmation Questions: FORCE

This command-line flag makes PGP assume "yes" for the user response to the confirmation request to overwrite an existing file, or when removing a key from the keyring via the '-kr' command.

Here is an example of how to set this flag:

pgp +force *cipherfile*

or:

pgp -kr +force Smith

This feature is useful for running PGP non-interactively from a Unix shell script or MSDOS batch file.

PGP Returns Exit Status to the Shell

To facilitate running PGP in "batch" mode, such as from an MSDOS '.bat' file or from a Unix shell script, PGP returns an error exit status to the shell. An exit status code of zero means normal exit, while a nonzero exit status indicates some kind of error occurred. Different error exit conditions return different exit status codes to the shell.

Environmental Variable for Pass Phrase

Normally, PGP prompts the user to type a pass phrase whenever PGP needs a pass phrase to unlock a secret key. But it is possible to store the pass phrase in an environmental variable from your operating system's command shell. The environmental variable PGPPASS can be used to hold the pass phrase that PGP will attempt to use first. If the pass phrase stored in PGPPASS is incorrect, PGP recovers by prompting the user for the correct pass phrase.

For example, in MSDOS, the shell command:

SET PGPPASS=zaphod beeblebrox for president

would eliminate the prompt for the pass phrase if the pass phrase were indeed "zaphod beeblebrox for president".

This dangerous feature makes your life more convenient if you have to regularly deal with a large number of incoming messages addressed to your secret key, by eliminating the need for you to repeatedly type in your pass phrase every time you run PGP.

I added this feature because of popular demand. However, this is a somewhat dangerous feature, because it keeps your precious pass phrase stored somewhere other than just in your brain. Even worse, if you are particularly reckless, it may even be stored on a disk on the same computer as your secret key. It would be particularly dangerous and stupid if you were to install this command in a batch or script file, such as the MSDOS 'AUTOEXEC.BAT' file. Someone could come along on your lunch hour and steal both your secret key ring and the file containing your pass phrase.

I can't emphasize the importance of this risk enough. If you are contemplating using this feature, be sure to read the sections "Exposure on Multi-user Systems" in chapter 11 and "How to Protect Secret Keys from Disclosure" in chapter 5.

If you must use this feature, the safest way to do it would be to just manually type in the shell command to set PGPPASS every time you boot your machine to start using PGP, and then erase it or turn off your machine when you are done. And you should definitely never do it in an environment where someone else may have access to your machine. Someone could come along and simply ask your computer to display the contents of PGPPASS.

Sometimes you want to pass the pass phrase into PGP from another application, such as an email package. In some cases, it may not always be desirable to use the PGPPASS variable for that purpose. There is another way to pass your pass phrase into PGP from another application. Use the '-z' command line option. This option is designed primarily for invoking PGP from inside an email package. The pass phrase follows the '-z' option on the command line. There are risks associated with using this approach, similar to those risks described above for using the PGPPASS variable.

9

Setting Configuration Parameters

PGP has a number of user-settable parameters that can be defined in a special PGP configuration text file called 'config.txt', in the directory pointed to by the shell environmental variable PGPPATH. Having a configuration file enables the user to define various flags and parameters for PGP without the burden of having to always define these parameters in the PGP command line.

The filename 'config.txt' has been in use for a long time by PGP, but some folks have pointed out that it may be at odds with naming conventions for configuration files for specific operating systems. Accordingly, PGP now tries to open this filename only after first trying to open the file '.pgprc' on Unix platforms, and 'pgp.ini' on other platforms, in the same directory that PGP would look for 'config.txt'.

Configuration parameters may be assigned integer values, character string values, or on/off values, depending on what kind of configuration parameter it is. A sample configuration file is provided with PGP, so you can see some examples.

In the configuration file, blank lines are ignored, as is anything following the '#' comment character. Keywords are not case-sensitive.

Here is a short sample fragment of a typical configuration file:

```
# TMP is the directory for PGP scratch files,
# such as a RAM disk.
TMP = "e:\"       # Can be overridden by
                  # environment variable TMP.
```

```
Armor = on          # Use -a flag for ASCII armor
                    # whenever applicable.
# CERT_DEPTH is how deeply introducers may
# introduce introducers.
cert_depth = 3
```

If some configuration parameters are not defined in the configuration file, or if there is no configuration file, or if PGP can't find the configuration file, the values for the configuration parameters default to some reasonable value.

Note that it is also possible to set these same configuration parameters directly from the PGP command line, by preceding the parameter setting with a '+' character. For example, the following two PGP commands produce the same effect:

```
pgp -e +armor=on message.txt smith
```

or:

```
pgp -ea message.txt smith
```

The following is a summary of the various parameters than may be defined in the configuration file.

TMP—Directory Pathname for Temporary Files

Default setting: TMP = " "
The configuration parameter TMP specifies what directory to use for PGP's temporary scratch files. The best place to put them is on a RAM disk, if you have one. That speeds things up quite a bit, and increases security somewhat. If TMP is undefined, the temporary files go in the current directory. If the shell environmental variable TMP is defined, PGP instead uses that to specify where the temporary files should go.

LANGUAGE—Language Selector

Default setting: LANGUAGE = "en"
PGP displays various prompts, warning messages, and advisories to the user on the screen. For example, messages such as "File not

found.", or "Please enter your pass phrase:". These messages are normally in English. But it is possible to get PGP to display its messages to the user in other languages, without having to modify the PGP executable program.

A number of people in various countries have translated all of PGP's display messages, warnings, and prompts into their native languages. These hundreds of translated message strings have been placed in a special text file called "language.txt", distributed with the PGP release. The messages are stored in this file in English, Spanish, Dutch, German, French, Italian, Russian, Latvian, and Lithuanian. Other languages may be added later.

The configuration parameter LANGUAGE specifies what language to display these messages in. LANGUAGE may be set to `"en"` for English, `"es"` for Spanish, `"de"` for German, `"nl"` for Dutch, `"fr"` for French, `"it"` for Italian, `"ru"` for Russian, `"lt3"` for Lithuanian, `"lv"` for Latvian, `"esp"` for Esperanto. For example, if this line appeared in the configuration file:

```
LANGUAGE = "fr"
```

PGP would select French as the language for its display messages. The default setting is English.

When PGP needs to display a message to the user, it looks in the 'language.txt' file for the equivalent message string in the selected foreign language and displays that translated message to the user. If PGP can't find the language string file, or if the selected language is not in the file, or if that one phrase is not translated into the selected language in the file, or if that phrase is missing entirely from the file, PGP displays the message in English.

To conserve disk space, most foreign translations are not included in the standard PGP release package, but are available separately.

MYNAME—Default User ID for Making Signatures

Default setting: MYNAME = `" "`

The configuration parameter MYNAME specifies the default user ID to use to select the secret key for making signatures. If MYNAME is not defined, the most recent secret key you installed on your secret key ring will be used. The user may also override this setting by specifying a user ID on the PGP command line with the '-u' option.

TEXTMODE—Assuming Plaintext Is a Text File

Default setting: TEXTMODE = off

The configuration parameter TEXTMODE is equivalent to the '-t' command line option. If enabled, it causes PGP to assume the plaintext is a text file, not a binary file, and converts it to "canonical text" before encrypting it. Canonical text has a carriage return and a linefeed at the end of each line of text.

This mode will be automatically turned off if PGP detects that the plaintext file contains what it thinks is non-text binary data. If you intend to use PGP primarily for email purposes, you should turn TEXTMODE = on.

For VAX/VMS systems, the current version of PGP defaults TEXTMODE = on.

For further details, see the section "Sending ASCII Text Files across Different Machine Environments" in chapter 8.

CHARSET—Specifies Local Character Set for Text Files

Default setting: CHARSET = NOCONV

Because PGP must process messages in many non-English languages with non-ASCII character sets, you may have a need to tell PGP what local character set your machine uses. This determines what character conversions are performed when converting plaintext files to and from canonical text format. This is only a concern if you are in a non-English non-ASCII environment.

The configuration parameter CHARSET selects the local character set. The choices are NOCONV (no conversion), LATIN1 (ISO 8859-1 Latin Alphabet 1), KOI8 (used by most Russian Unix systems), ALT_CODES (used by Russian MSDOS systems), ASCII, and CP850 (used by most western European languages on standard MSDOS PCs).

LATIN1 is the internal representation used by PGP for canonical text, so if you select LATIN1, no conversion is done. Note also that

PGP treats KOI8 as LATIN1, even though it is a completely different character set (Russian), because trying to convert KOI8 to either LATIN1 or CP850 would be futile anyway. This means that setting CHARSET to NOCONV, LATIN1, or KOI8 are all equivalent to PGP.

If you use MSDOS and expect to send or receive traffic in western European languages, set CHARSET = "CP850". This will make PGP convert incoming canonical text messages from LATIN1 to CP850 after decryption. If you use the '-t' (textmode) option to convert to canonical text, PGP will convert your CP850 text to LATIN1 before encrypting it.

For further details, see the section "Sending ASCII Text Files across Different Machine Environments" in chapter 8.

ARMOR—Enable ASCII Armor Output

Default setting: ARMOR = off

The configuration parameter ARMOR is equivalent to the '-a' command line option. If enabled, it causes PGP to emit ciphertext or keys in ASCII radix-64 format suitable for transporting through email channels. Output files are named with the '.asc' extension.

If you intend to use PGP primarily for email purposes, you should turn ARMOR = on.

For further details, see the section "Sending Ciphertext through Email Channels" in chapter 6.

ARMORLINES—Size of ASCII Armor Multipart Files

Default setting: ARMORLINES = 720

When PGP creates a very large '.asc' radix-64 file for sending ciphertext or keys through the email, it breaks the file up into separate chunks small enough to send through Internet mail utilities. Normally, Internet mailers prohibit files larger than about 50,000 bytes, which means that if we restrict the number of lines to about 720, we'll be well within the limit. The file chunks are named with suffixes 'as1', 'as2', 'as3', and so on.

The configuration parameter ARMORLINES specifies the maximum number of lines to make each chunk in a multipart '.asc' file sequence. If you set it to zero, PGP will not break up the file into chunks.

Fidonet email files usually have an upper limit of about 32K bytes, so 450 lines would be appropriate for Fidonet environments.

For further details, see the section "Sending Ciphertext through Email Channels" in chapter 6.

KEEPBINARY—Keep Binary Ciphertext Files after Decrypting

Default setting: KEEPBINARY = off

When PGP reads a '.asc' file, it recognizes that the file is in radix-64 format and will convert it back to binary before processing as it normally does, producing as a by-product a '.pgp' ciphertext file in binary form. After further processing to decrypt the '.pgp' file, the final output file will be in normal plaintext form.

You may want to delete the binary '.pgp' intermediate file, or you may want PGP to delete it for you automatically. You can still rerun PGP on the original '.asc' file.

The configuration parameter KEEPBINARY enables or disables keeping the intermediate '.pgp' file during decryption.

For further details, see the section "Sending Ciphertext through Email Channels" in chapter 6.

COMPRESS—Enable Compression

Default setting: COMPRESS = on

The configuration parameter COMPRESS enables or disables data compression before encryption. It is used mainly for debugging PGP. Normally, PGP attempts to compress the plaintext before it encrypts it. Generally, you should leave this alone and let PGP attempt to compress the plaintext.

COMPLETES_NEEDED—Number of Completely Trusted Introducers Needed

Default setting: COMPLETES_NEEDED = 1

The configuration parameter COMPLETES_NEEDED specifies the minimum number of completely trusted introducers required to fully certify a public key on your public key ring. This gives you a way of tuning PGP's skepticism.

For further details, see the section "How Does PGP Keep Track of Which Keys Are Valid?" in chapter 5.

MARGINALS_NEEDED—Number of Marginally Trusted Introducers Needed

Default setting: MARGINALS_NEEDED = 2

The configuration parameter MARGINALS_NEEDED specifies the minimum number of marginally trusted introducers required to fully certify a public key on your public key ring. This gives you a way of tuning PGP's skepticism.

For further details, see the section "How Does PGP Keep Track of Which Keys Are Valid?" in chapter 5.

CERT_DEPTH—How Deep May Introducers Be Nested?

Default setting: CERT_DEPTH = 4

The configuration parameter CERT_DEPTH specifies how many levels deep you may nest introducers to certify other introducers to certify public keys on your public key ring. For example, if CERT_DEPTH is set to 1, there may only be one layer of introducers below your own ultimately-trusted key. If that were the case, you would be required to directly certify the public keys of all trusted introducers on your key ring. If you set CERT_DEPTH to 0, you could have no introducers at all, and you would have to directly certify each and every key on your public key ring in order to use it. The minimum CERT_DEPTH is 0, the maximum is 8.

For further details, see the section "How Does PGP Keep Track of Which Keys Are Valid?" in chapter 5.

BAKRING—Filename for Backup Secret Keyring

Default setting: BAKRING = " "

All of the key certification that PGP does on your public key ring ultimately depends on your own ultimately-trusted public key (or keys). To detect any tampering of your public key ring, PGP must check that your own key has not been tampered with. To do this, PGP must compare your public key against a backup copy of your secret key on some tamper-resistant media, such as a write-protected floppy disk. A secret key contains all the information that your public key has, plus some secret components. This means PGP can check your public key against a backup copy of your secret key.

The configuration parameter BAKRING specifies what pathname to use for PGP's trusted backup copy of your secret key ring. On MSDOS, you could set it to 'a:\secring.pgp' to point it at a write-protected backup copy of your secret key ring on your floppy drive. This check is performed only when you execute the PGP '-kc' option to check your whole public key ring.

If BAKRING is not defined, PGP will not check your own key against any backup copy.

See the sections "How to Protect Public Keys from Tampering" and "How Does PGP Keep Track of Which Keys Are Valid?" in chapter 5.

PUBRING—Filename for Your Public Keyring

Default setting: PUBRING = "$PGPPATH/pubring.pgp"

You may want to keep your public keyring in a directory separate from your PGP configuration file in the directory specified by your $PGPPATH environmental variable. You may specify the full path and filename for your public keyring by setting the PUBRING parameter. For example, on an MSDOS system, you might want to keep your public keyring on a floppy disk by:

```
PUBRING = "a:pubring.pgp"
```

This feature is especially handy for specifying an alternative keyring on the command line.

SECRING—Filename for Your Secret Keyring

Default setting: SECRING = "$PGPPATH/secring.pgp"

You may want to keep your secret keyring in a directory separate from your PGP configuration file in the directory specified by your $PGPPATH environmental variable. This comes in handy for putting your secret keyring in a directory or device that is more protected than your public keyring. You may specify the full path and filename for your secret keyring by setting the SECRING parameter. For example, on an MSDOS system, you might want to keep your secret keyring on a floppy disk by:

SECRING = "a:secring.pgp"

RANDSEED—Filename for Random Number Seed

Default setting: RANDSEED = "$PGPPATH/randseed.bin"

You may want to keep your random number seed file (for generation of session keys) in a directory separate from your PGP configuration file in the directory specified by your $PGPPATH environmental variable. This comes in handy for putting your random number seed file in a directory or device that is more protected than your public keyring. You may specify the full path and filename for your random seed file by setting the RANDSEED parameter. For example, on an MSDOS system, you might want to keep it on a floppy disk by:

RANDSEED = "a:randseed.bin"

PAGER—Selects Shell Command to Display Plaintext Output

Default setting: PAGER = " "

PGP lets you view the decrypted plaintext output on your screen (like the Unix-style more command), without writing it to a file, if you use the '-m' (more) option while decrypting. This displays the decrypted plaintext display on your screen one screenful at a time.

If you prefer to use a fancier page display utility, rather than PGP's built-in one, you can specify the name of a shell command that PGP will invoke to display your plaintext output file. The configuration parameter PAGER specifies the shell command to invoke to display the file. For example, on MSDOS systems, you might want to use the popular shareware program 'list.com' to display your plaintext message. Assuming you have a copy of 'list.com', you may set PAGER accordingly:

PAGER = "list"

For further details, see the section "Displaying Decrypted Plaintext on Your Screen" in chapter 8.

SHOWPASS—Echo Pass Phrase to User

Default setting: SHOWPASS = off

Normally, PGP does not let you see your pass phrase as you type it in. This makes it harder for someone to look over your shoulder while you type and learn your pass phrase. But some typing-impaired people have problems typing their pass phrase without seeing what they are typing, and they may be typing in the privacy of their own homes. So they asked if PGP can be configured to let them see what they type when they type in their pass phrase.

The configuration parameter SHOWPASS enables PGP to echo your typing during pass phrase entry.

TZFIX—Timezone Adjustment

Default setting: TZFIX = 0

PGP provides timestamps for keys and signature certificates in Greenwich Mean Time (GMT), or Coordinated Universal Time (UTC), which means the same thing for our purposes. When PGP asks the system for the time of day, the system is supposed to provide it in GMT.

But sometimes, because of improperly configured MSDOS systems, the system time is returned in U.S. Pacific Standard Time time plus 8 hours. Sounds weird, doesn't it? Perhaps because of some sort of U.S. west-coast jingoism, MSDOS presumes local time is U.S. Pacific time, and pre-corrects Pacific time to GMT. This adversely affects the behavior of the internal MSDOS GMT time function that PGP calls. However, if your MSDOS environmental variable TZ is already properly defined for your timezone, this corrects the misconception MSDOS has that the whole world lives on the U.S. west coast.

The configuration parameter TZFIX specifies the number of hours to add to the system time function to get GMT, for GMT timestamps on keys and signatures. If the MSDOS environmental variable TZ is defined properly, you can leave TZFIX = 0. Unix systems usually shouldn't need to worry about setting TZFIX at all. But if you are using some other obscure operating system that doesn't know about GMT, you may have to use TZFIX to adjust the system time to GMT.

On MSDOS systems that do not have TZ defined in the environment, you should make TZFIX = 0 for California, -1 for Colorado, -2 for Chicago, -3 for New York, -8 for London, -9 for Amsterdam. In the summer, TZFIX should be manually decremented from these values. What a mess.

It would be much cleaner to set your MSDOS environmental variable TZ in your 'AUTOEXEC.BAT' file, and not use the TZFIX correction. Then MSDOS gives you good GMT timestamps, and will handle daylight savings time adjustments for you. Here are some sample lines to insert into 'AUTOEXEC.BAT', depending on your time zone:

For Los Angeles:	SET TZ=PST8PDT
For Denver:	SET TZ=MST7MDT
For Arizona:	SET TZ=MST7
(Arizona never uses daylight savings time)	
For Chicago:	SET TZ=CST6CDT
For New York:	SET TZ=EST5EDT
For London:	SET TZ=GMT0BST
For Amsterdam:	SET TZ=MET-1DST
For Moscow:	SET TZ=MSK-3MSD
For Aukland:	SET TZ=NZT-13

CLEARSIG—Enable Signed Messages to Be Encapsulated as Clear Text

Default setting: CLEARSIG = on

Normally, unencrypted PGP signed messages have a signature certificate prepended in binary form. Also, the signed message is compressed, rendering the message unreadable to casual human eyes, even though the message is not actually encrypted. To send this binary data through a 7-bit email channel, radix-64 ASCII armor is applied (see the ARMOR parameter). Even if PGP didn't compress the message, the ASCII armor would still render the message unreadable to human eyes. The recipient must use PGP to strip the armor off and decompress it before reading the message.

If the original plaintext message is in text (not binary) form, there is a way to send a signed message through an email channel in such a way that the signed message is not compressed and the ASCII armor is applied only to the binary signature certificate, but not to the plaintext message. The CLEARSIG flag provides this useful feature, making it possible to generate a signed message that can be read with human eyes, without the aid of PGP. Of course, you still need PGP to actually check the signature.

The CLEARSIG flag is preset to on beginning with PGP version 2.5. To enable the full CLEARSIG behavior, the ARMOR and TEXTMODE flags must also be turned on. Set ARMOR = on (or use the '-a' option), and set TEXTMODE = on (or use the '-t' option). If your config file has CLEARSIG turned off, you can turn it back on again directly on the command line, like so:

```
pgp -sta +clearsig=on message.txt
```

This message representation is analogous to the MIC-CLEAR message type used in Internet Privacy Enhanced Mail (PEM). It is important to note that since this method only applies ASCII armor to the binary signature certificate, and not to the message text itself, there is some risk that the unarmored message may suffer some accidental molestation while en route. This can happen if it passes through some email gateway that performs character set conversions, or in some cases extra spaces may be added to or stripped from the ends of lines. If this occurs, the signature will fail to verify, which may give a false indication of intentional tampering. But since PEM lives under a similar vulnerability, it seems worth having this feature despite the risks.

Beginning with PGP version 2.2, trailing blanks are ignored on each line in calculating the signature for text in CLEARSIG mode.

VERBOSE—Quiet, Normal, or Verbose Messages

Default setting: VERBOSE = 1

VERBOSE may be set to 0, 1, or 2, depending on how much detail you want to see from PGP diagnostic messages. The settings are:

0   Display messages only if there is a problem. Unix fans wanted this "quiet mode" setting.

1   Normal default setting. Displays a reasonable amount of detail in diagnostic or advisory messages.

2   Displays maximum information, usually to help diagnose problems in PGP. Not recommended for normal use. Besides, PGP doesn't have any problems, right?

INTERACTIVE—Ask for Confirmation for Key Adds

Default Setting: INTERACTIVE = off
Enabling this mode will mean that if you add a key file containing multiple keys to your key ring, PGP will ask for confirmation for each key before adding it to your key ring.

NOMANUAL—Let PGP Generate Keys without the Manual

Default Setting: NOMANUAL = off
It is important that the freeware version of PGP not be distributed without the user documentation, which normally comes with it in the standard release package. This manual contains important information for using PGP, as well as important legal notices. But some people have distributed previous versions of PGP without the manual, causing a lot of problems for a lot of people who get it. To discourage the distribution of PGP without the required documentation, PGP has been changed to require the *PGP User's Guide* to be found somewhere on your computer (like in your PGP directory) before PGP will let you generate a key pair. However, some users like to use PGP on tiny palmtop computers with limited storage capacity, so they like to run PGP without the documentation present on their systems. To satisfy these users, PGP can be made to relax its requirement that the manual be present, by enabling the NOMANUAL flag on the command line during key generation, like so:

```
pgp -kg +nomanual
```

The NOMANUAL flag can only be set on the command line, not in the config file. Since you must read this manual to learn how to enable this simple override feature, I hope this will still be effective in discouraging the distribution of PGP without the manual.

Some people may object to PGP insisting on finding the manual somewhere in the neighborhood to generate a key. They bristle against this seemingly authoritarian attitude. Some people have even modified PGP to defeat this feature, and redistributed their hotwired version to others. That creates problems for me. Before I added this feature, there were maimed versions of the PGP distribution package floating around that lacked the manual. One of them was uploaded to Compuserve, and was distributed to countless users who called me on the phone to ask me why such a complicated program had no manual. It spread out to BBS systems around the country. And a freeware distributor got hold of the package from Compuserve and enshrined it on CD-ROM, distributing thousands of copies without the manual. What a mess.

10

A Peek under the Hood

Let's take a look at a few internal features of PGP.

Random Numbers

PGP uses a cryptographically strong pseudorandom number generator for creating temporary conventional session keys. The seed file for this is called 'randseed.bin'. It too can be kept in whatever directory is indicated by the PGPPATH environmental variable. If this random seed file does not exist, it is automatically created and seeded with truly random numbers derived from timing your keystroke latencies.

This generator reseeds the disk file each time it is used by mixing in new key material partially derived with the time of day and other truly random sources. It uses the conventional encryption algorithm as an engine for the random number generator. The seed file contains both random seed material and random key material to key the conventional encryption engine for the random generator.

This random seed file should be at least slightly protected from disclosure, to reduce the risk of an attacker deriving your next or previous session keys. The attacker would have a very hard time getting anything useful from capturing this random seed file, because the file is cryptographically laundered before and after each use. Nonetheless, it seems prudent to at least try to keep it from falling into the wrong hands.

If you feel uneasy about trusting any algorithmically derived random number source however strong, keep in mind that you already trust the strength of the same conventional cipher to protect your messages. If it's strong enough for that, then it should be strong enough to use as a source of random numbers for temporary session keys. Note that PGP still uses truly random numbers from physical sources (mainly keyboard timings) to generate long-term public/secret key pairs.

Conventional Encryption

As described earlier, PGP "bootstraps" into a conventional single-key encryption algorithm by using a public key algorithm to encipher the conventional session key and then switching to fast conventional cryptography. So let's talk about this conventional encryption algorithm. It isn't the DES.

The Federal Data Encryption Standard (DES) used to be a good algorithm for most commercial applications. But the government never did trust the DES to protect its own classified data, because the DES key length is only 56 bits, short enough for a brute force attack. Also, the full 16-round DES has been attacked with some success by Biham and Shamir using differential cryptanalysis, and by Matsui using linear cryptanalysis.

The most devastating practical attack on the DES was described at the Crypto '93 conference, where Michael Wiener of Bell Northern Research presented a paper on how to crack the DES with a special machine. He has fully designed and tested a chip that guesses 50 million DES keys per second until it finds the right one. Although he has refrained from building the real chips so far, he can get these chips manufactured for $10.50 each, and can build 57000 of them into a special machine for $1 million that can try every DES key in 7 hours, averaging a solution in 3.5 hours. $1 million can be hidden in the budget of many companies. For $10 million, it takes 21 minutes to crack, and for $100 million, just two minutes. With any major government's budget for examining DES traffic, it can be cracked in seconds. This means that straight 56-bit DES is now effectively dead for purposes of serious data security applications.

A possible successor to DES may be a variation known as "triple DES", which uses two DES keys to encrypt three times, achieving an effective key space of 112 bits. But this approach is three times slower than normal DES. A future version of PGP may support triple DES as an option.

PGP does not use the DES as its conventional single-key algorithm to encrypt messages. Instead, PGP uses a different conventional single-key block encryption algorithm, called IDEA™.

For the cryptographically curious, the IDEA cipher has a 64-bit block size for the plaintext and the ciphertext. It uses a key size of 128 bits. It is based on the design concept of "mixing operations from different algebraic groups". It runs much faster in software than the DES. Like the DES, it can be used in cipher feedback (CFB) and cipher block chaining (CBC) modes. PGP uses it in 64-bit CFB mode.

The IPES/IDEA block cipher was developed at ETH in Zurich by James L. Massey and Xuejia Lai, and published in 1990. This is not a "home-grown" algorithm. Its designers have a distinguished reputation in the cryptologic community. Early published papers on the algorithm called it IPES (Improved Proposed Encryption Standard), but they later changed the name to IDEA (International Data Encryption Algorithm). So far, IDEA has resisted attack much better than other ciphers such as FEAL, REDOC-II, LOKI, Snefru and Khafre. And recent evidence suggests that IDEA is more resistant than the DES to Biham & Shamir's highly successful differential cryptanalysis attack. Biham and Shamir have been examining the IDEA cipher for weaknesses, without success. Academic cryptanalyst groups in Belgium, England, and Germany are also attempting to attack it, as well as the military services from several European countries. As this new cipher continues to attract attack efforts from the most formidable quarters of the cryptanalytic world, confidence in IDEA is growing with the passage of time.

Every once in a while, I get a letter from someone who has just learned the awful truth that PGP does not use pure RSA to encrypt bulk data. They are concerned that the whole package is weakened if we use a hybrid public-key and conventional scheme just to speed things up. After all, a chain is only as strong as its weakest link. They demand an explanation for this apparent "compromise" in the strength of PGP. This may be because they have been caught up in the public's reverence and awe for the strength and mystique of

RSA, mistakenly believing that RSA is intrinsically stronger than any conventional cipher. Well, it's not.

People who work in factoring research say that the workload to exhaust all the possible 128-bit keys in the IDEA cipher would roughly equal the factoring workload to crack a 3100-bit RSA key, which is quite a bit bigger than the 1024-bit RSA key size that most people use for high security applications. Given this range of key sizes, and assuming there are no hidden weaknesses in the conventional cipher, the weak link in this hybrid approach is in the public key algorithm, not the conventional cipher.

It is not ergonomically practical to use pure RSA with large keys to encrypt and decrypt long messages. A 1024-bit RSA key would decrypt messages about 4000 times slower than the IDEA cipher. Absolutely no one does it that way in the real world. Many people less experienced in cryptography do not realize that the attraction of public key cryptography is not that it is intrinsically stronger than a conventional cipher—its appeal is that it helps you manage keys more conveniently.

Not only is RSA too slow to use on bulk data, but it even has certain weaknesses that can be exploited in some special cases of particular kinds of messages that are fed to the RSA cipher, even for large keys. These special cases can be avoided by using the hybrid approach of using RSA to encrypt random session keys for a conventional cipher, like PGP does. So the bottom line is this: Using pure RSA on bulk data is the wrong approach, period. It's too slow, it's not stronger, and may even be weaker. If you find a software application that uses pure RSA on bulk data, it probably means the implementor does not understand these issues, which could imply he doesn't understand other important concepts of cryptography.

Data Compression

PGP normally compresses the plaintext before encrypting it. It's too late to compress it after it has been encrypted; encrypted data is incompressible. Data compression saves modem transmission time and disk space and more importantly strengthens cryptographic security. Most cryptanalysis techniques exploit redundancies found in the plaintext to crack the cipher. Data compression reduces this redundancy in the plaintext, thereby greatly enhancing resistance to cryptanalysis. It takes extra time to compress the plaintext, but from a security point of view it seems worth it, at least in my cautious opinion.

Files that are too short to compress or just don't compress well are not compressed by PGP.

If you prefer, you can use PKZIP to compress the plaintext before encrypting it. PKZIP is a widely-available and effective MSDOS shareware compression utility from PKWare, Inc. Or you can use ZIP, a PKZIP-compatible freeware compression utility on Unix and other systems, available from Jean-loup Gailly. There is some advantage in using PKZIP or ZIP in certain cases, because unlike PGP's built-in compression algorithm, PKZIP and ZIP have the nice feature of compressing multiple files into a single compressed file, which is reconstituted again into separate files when decompressed. PGP will not try to compress a plaintext file that has already been compressed. After decrypting, the recipient can decompress the plaintext with PKUNZIP. If the decrypted plaintext is a PKZIP compressed file, PGP automatically recognizes this and advises the recipient that the decrypted plaintext appears to be a PKZIP file.

For the technically curious readers, the current version of PGP uses the freeware ZIP compression routines written by Jean-loup Gailly, Mark Adler, and Richard B. Wales. This ZIP software uses functionally-equivalent compression algorithms as those used by PKWare's new PKZIP 2.0. This ZIP compression software was selected for PGP mainly because of its free portable C source code availability, and because it has a really good compression ratio, and because it's fast.

Peter Gutmann has also written a nice compression utility called HPACK, available for free from many Internet FTP sites. It encrypts the compressed archives, using PGP data formats and key rings. He wanted me to mention that here.

Message Digests and Digital Signatures

To create a digital signature, PGP encrypts with your secret key. But PGP doesn't actually encrypt your entire message with your secret key—that would take too long. Instead, PGP encrypts a message digest.

The *message digest* is a compact (128 bit) "distillate" of your message, similar in concept to a checksum. You can also think of it as a "fingerprint" of the message. The message digest "represents" your message, such that if the message were altered in any way, a different message digest would be computed from it. This makes it possible to detect any changes made to the message by a forger. A message digest is computed using a cryptographically strong one-way hash function of the message. It would be computationally infeasible for an attacker to devise a substitute message that would produce an identical message digest. In that respect, a message digest is much better than a checksum, because it is easy to devise a different message that would produce the same checksum. But like a checksum, you can't derive the original message from its message digest.

A message digest alone is not enough to authenticate a message. The message digest algorithm is publicly known, and does not require knowledge of any secret keys to calculate. If all we did was attach a message digest to a message, then a forger could alter a message and simply attach a new message digest calculated from the new altered message. To provide real authentication, the sender has to encrypt (sign) the message digest with his secret key.

A message digest is calculated from the message by the sender. The sender's secret key is used to encrypt the message digest and an electronic timestamp, forming a digital signature, or signature certificate. The sender sends the digital signature along with the message. The receiver receives the message and the digital signature, and recovers the original message digest from the digital signature by decrypting it with the sender's public key. The receiver computes a new message digest from the message, and checks to see if it matches the one recovered from the digital signature. If it matches, then that proves the message was not altered, and it came from the sender who owns the public key used to check the signature.

A potential forger would have to either produce an altered message that produces an identical message digest (which is infeasible), or he would have to create a new digital signature from a different message digest (also infeasible, without knowing the true sender's secret key).

Digital signatures prove who sent the message, and that the message was not altered either by error or design. It also provides non-repudiation, which means the sender cannot easily disavow his signature on the message.

Using message digests to form digital signatures has other advantages besides being faster than directly signing the entire actual message with the secret key. Using message digests allows signatures to be of a standard small fixed size, regardless of the size of the actual message. It also allows the software to check the message integrity automatically, in a manner similar to using checksums. And it allows signatures to be stored separately from messages, perhaps even in a public archive, without revealing sensitive information about the actual messages, because no one can derive any message content from a message digest.

The message digest algorithm used here is the MD5 Message Digest Algorithm, placed in the public domain by RSA Data Security, Inc. MD5's designer, Ronald Rivest, writes this about MD5:

It is conjectured that the difficulty of coming up with two messages having the same message digest is on the order of 2^{64} operations, and that the difficulty of coming up with any message having a given message digest is on the order of 2^{128} operations. The MD5 algorithm has been carefully scrutinized for weaknesses. It is, however, a relatively new algorithm and further security analysis is of course justified, as is the case with any new proposal of this sort. The level of security provided by MD5 should be sufficient for implementing very high security hybrid digital signature schemes based on MD5 and the RSA public-key cryptosystem.

11

Vulnerabilities

No data security system is impenetrable. PGP can be circumvented in a variety of ways. In any data security system, you have to ask yourself if the information you are trying to protect is more valuable to your attacker than the cost of the attack. This should lead you to protecting yourself from the cheapest attacks, while not worrying about the more expensive attacks.

Some of the discussion that follows may seem unduly paranoid, but such an attitude is appropriate for a reasonable discussion of vulnerability issues.

Compromised Pass Phrase and Secret Key

Probably the simplest attack is if you leave your pass phrase for your secret key written down somewhere. If someone gets it and also gets your secret key file, they can read your messages and make signatures in your name.

Don't use obvious passwords that can be easily guessed, such as the names of your kids or spouse. If you make your pass phrase a single word, it can be easily guessed by having a computer try all the words in the dictionary until it finds your password. That's why a pass phrase is so much better than a password. A more sophisticated attacker may have his computer scan a book of famous quotations to find your pass phrase. An easy to remember but hard to guess pass phrase can be easily constructed by some creatively nonsensical sayings or very obscure literary quotes.

For further details, see the section "How to Protect Secret Keys from Disclosure" in chapter 5.

Public Key Tampering

A major vulnerability exists if public keys are tampered with. This may be the most crucially important vulnerability of a public key cryptosystem, in part because most novices don't immediately recognize it. The importance of this vulnerability, and appropriate hygienic countermeasures, are detailed in the section "How to Protect Public Keys from Tampering" in chapter 5.

To summarize: When you use someone's public key, make certain it has not been tampered with. A new public key from someone else should be trusted only if you got it directly from its owner, or if it has been signed by someone you trust. Make sure no one else can tamper with your own public key ring. Maintain physical control of both your public key ring and your secret key ring, preferably on your own personal computer rather than on a remote timesharing system. Keep a backup copy of both key rings.

"Not Quite Deleted" Files

Another potential security problem is caused by how most operating systems delete files. When you encrypt a file and then delete the original plaintext file, the operating system doesn't actually physically erase the data. It merely marks those disk blocks as deleted, allowing the space to be reused later. It's sort of like discarding sensitive paper documents in the paper recycling bin instead of the paper shredder. The disk blocks still contain the original sensitive data you wanted to erase, and will probably eventually be overwritten by new data at some point in the future. If an attacker reads these deleted disk blocks soon after they have been deallocated, he could recover your plaintext.

In fact this could even happen accidentally, if for some reason something went wrong with the disk and some files were accidentally deleted or corrupted. A disk recovery program may be run to recover the damaged files, but this often means some previously deleted files are resurrected along with everything else. Your confidential files that you thought were gone forever could then reappear and be inspected by whomever is attempting to recover your damaged disk. Even while you are creating the original message with a word processor or text editor, the editor may be creating multiple temporary copies of your text on the disk, just because of its internal workings. These temporary copies of your text are deleted by the word processor when it's done, but these sensitive fragments are still on your disk somewhere.

Let me tell you a true horror story. I had a friend, married with young children, who once had a brief and not very serious affair. She wrote a letter to her lover on her word processor, and deleted the letter after she sent it. Later, after the affair was over, the floppy disk got damaged somehow and she had to recover it because it contained other important documents. She asked her husband to salvage the disk, which seemed perfectly safe because she knew she had deleted the incriminating letter. Her husband ran a commercial disk recovery software package to salvage the files. It recovered the files alright, including the deleted letter. He read it, which set off a tragic chain of events.

The only way to prevent the plaintext from reappearing is to somehow cause the deleted plaintext files to be overwritten. Unless you know for sure that all the deleted disk blocks will soon be reused, you must take positive steps to overwrite the plaintext file, and also any fragments of it on the disk left by your word processor. You can overwrite the original plaintext file after encryption by using the PGP '-w' (wipe) option. You can take care of any fragments of the plaintext left on the disk by using any of the disk utilities available that can overwrite all of the unused blocks on a disk. For example, the Norton Utilities for MSDOS can do this.

Even if you overwrite the plaintext data on the disk, it may still be possible for a resourceful and determined attacker to recover the data. Faint magnetic traces of the original data remain on the disk after it has been overwritten. Special sophisticated disk recovery hardware can sometimes be used to recover the data.

Viruses and Trojan Horses

Another attack could involve a specially-tailored hostile computer virus or worm that might infect PGP or your operating system. This hypothetical virus could be designed to capture your pass phrase or secret key or deciphered messages, and covertly write the captured information to a file or send it through a network to the virus's owner. Or it might alter PGP's behavior so that signatures are not properly checked. This attack is cheaper than cryptanalytic attacks.

Defending against this falls under the category of defending against viral infection generally. There are some moderately capable anti-viral products commercially available, and there are hygienic procedures to follow that can greatly reduce the chances of viral infection. A complete treatment of anti-viral and anti-worm countermeasures is beyond the scope of this document. PGP has no defenses against viruses, and assumes your own personal computer is a trustworthy execution environment. If such a virus or worm actually appeared, hopefully word would soon get around warning everyone.

Another similar attack involves someone creating a clever imitation of PGP that behaves like PGP in most respects, but doesn't work the way it's supposed to. For example, it might be deliberately crippled to not check signatures properly, allowing bogus key certificates to be accepted. This "Trojan horse" version of PGP is not hard for an attacker to create, because PGP source code is widely available, so anyone could modify the source code and produce a lobotomized zombie imitation PGP that looks real but does the bidding of its diabolical master. This Trojan horse version of PGP could then be widely circulated, claiming to be from me. How insidious.

You should make an effort to get your copy of PGP from a reliable source, whatever that means. Or perhaps from more than one independent source, and compare them with a file comparison utility.

There are other ways to check PGP for tampering, using digital signatures. If someone you trust signs the executable version of PGP, vouching for the fact that it has not been infected or tampered with, you can be reasonably sure that you have a good copy. You could use an earlier trusted version of PGP to check the signature on a later suspect version of PGP. But this will not help at all if your operating system is infected, nor will it detect if your original copy of 'PGP.EXE' has been maliciously altered in such a way as to compromise its own ability to check signatures. This test also assumes that you have a good trusted copy of the public key that you use to check the signature on the PGP executable.

I recommend you not trust your copy of PGP unless it was originally distributed by MIT or ViaCrypt, or unless it comes with a digitally signed endorsement from me. Every new version comes with one or more digital signatures in the distribution package, signed by the originator of that release package. This is usually someone representing MIT or ViaCrypt, or whoever released that version. Check the signatures on the version that you get. I have actually seen several bogus versions of PGP distribution packages, even from apparently reliable freeware distribution channels such as CD-ROM distributors and Compuserve. Always check the signature when you get a new version.

Physical Security Breach

A physical security breach may allow someone to physically acquire your plaintext files or printed messages. A determined opponent might accomplish this through burglary, trash-picking, unreasonable search and seizure, or bribery, blackmail or infiltration of your staff. Some of these attacks may be especially feasible against grassroots political organizations that depend on a largely volunteer staff. It has been widely reported in the press that the FBI's COINTELPRO program used burglary, infiltration, and illegal bugging against antiwar and civil rights groups. And look what happened at the Watergate Hotel.

Don't be lulled into a false sense of security just because you have a cryptographic tool. Cryptographic techniques protect data only while it's encrypted—direct physical security violations can still compromise plaintext data or written or spoken information.

This kind of attack is cheaper than cryptanalytic attacks on PGP.

Tempest Attacks

Another kind of attack that has been used by well-equipped opponents involves the remote detection of the electromagnetic signals from your computer. This expensive and somewhat labor-intensive attack is probably still cheaper than direct cryptanalytic attacks. An appropriately instrumented van can park near your office and remotely pick up all of your keystrokes and messages displayed on your computer video screen. This would compromise all of your passwords, messages, etc. This attack can be thwarted by properly shielding all of your computer equipment and network cabling so that it does not emit these signals. This shielding technology is known as "Tempest", and is used by some government agencies and defense contractors. There are hardware vendors who supply Tempest shielding commercially, although it may be subject to some kind of government licensing. Now why do you suppose the government would restrict access to Tempest shielding?

Exposure on Multi-user Systems

PGP was originally designed for a single-user MSDOS machine under your direct physical control. I run PGP at home on my own PC, and unless someone breaks into my house or monitors my electromagnetic emissions, they probably can't see my plaintext files or secret keys.

But now PGP also runs on multi-user systems such as Unix and VAX/VMS. On multi-user systems, there are much greater risks of your plaintext or keys or passwords being exposed. The Unix system administrator or a clever intruder can read your plaintext files, or perhaps even use special software to covertly monitor your keystrokes or read what's on your screen. On a Unix system, any other user can read your environment information remotely by simply using the Unix ps command. Similar problems exist for MSDOS machines connected on a local area network. The actual security risk is dependent on your particular situation. Some multi-user systems may be safe because all the users are trusted, or because they have system security measures that are safe enough to withstand the attacks available to the intruders, or because there just aren't any sufficiently interested intruders. Some Unix systems are safe because they are only used by one user—there are even some notebook computers running Unix. It would be unreasonable to simply exclude PGP from running on all Unix systems.

PGP is not designed to protect your data while it is in plaintext form on a compromised system. Nor can it prevent an intruder from using sophisticated measures to read your secret key while it is being used. You will just have to recognize these risks on multi-user systems, and adjust your expectations and behavior accordingly. Perhaps your situation is such that you should consider running PGP only on an isolated single-user system under your direct physical control. That's what I do, and that's what I recommend.

Traffic Analysis

Even if the attacker cannot read the contents of your encrypted messages, he may be able to infer at least some useful information by observing where the messages come from and where they are going, the size of the messages, and the time of day the messages are sent. This is analogous to the attacker looking at your long distance phone bill to see who you called and when and for how long, even though the actual content of your calls is unknown to the attacker. This is called traffic analysis. PGP alone does not protect against traffic analysis. Solving this problem would require specialized communication protocols designed to reduce exposure to traffic analysis in your communication environment, possibly with some cryptographic assistance.

Protecting against Bogus Timestamps

A somewhat obscure vulnerability of PGP involves dishonest users creating bogus timestamps on their own public key certificates and signatures. You can skip over this section if you are a casual user and aren't deeply into obscure public key protocols.

There's nothing to stop a dishonest user from altering the date and time setting of his own system's clock, and generating his own public key certificates and signatures that appear to have been created at a different time. He can make it appear that he signed something earlier or later than he actually did, or that his public/secret key pair was created earlier or later. This may have some legal or financial benefit to him, for example by creating some kind of loophole that might allow him to repudiate a signature.

I think this problem of falsified timestamps in digital signatures is no worse than it is already in handwritten signatures. Anyone may write a date next to their handwritten signature on a contract with any date they choose, yet no one seems to be alarmed over this state of affairs. In some cases, an "incorrect" date on a handwritten signature might not be associated with actual fraud. The timestamp might be when the signator asserts that he signed a document, or maybe when he wants the signature to go into effect.

In situations where it is critical that a signature be trusted to have the actual correct date, people can simply use notaries to witness and date a handwritten signature. The analog to this in digital signatures is to get a trusted third party to sign a signature certificate, applying a trusted timestamp. No exotic or overly formal protocols are needed for this. Witnessed signatures have long been recognized as a legitimate way of determining when a document was signed.

A trustworthy Certifying Authority or notary could create notarized signatures with a trustworthy timestamp. This would not necessarily require a centralized authority. Perhaps any trusted introducer or disinterested party could serve this function, the same way real notary publics do now. When a notary signs other people's signatures, it creates a signature certificate of a signature certificate. This would serve as a witness to the signature the same way real notaries now witness handwritten signatures. The notary could enter the detached signature certificate (without the actual whole document that was signed) into a special log controlled by the notary. Anyone can read this log. The notary's signature would have a trusted timestamp, which might have greater credibility or more legal significance than the timestamp in the original signature.

There is a good treatment of this topic in Denning's 1983 article in *IEEE Computer* (see the recommended readings in chapter 14). Future enhancements to PGP might have features to easily manage notarized signatures of signatures, with trusted timestamps.

Cryptanalysis

An expensive and formidable cryptanalytic attack could possibly be mounted by someone with vast supercomputer resources, such as a government intelligence agency. They might crack your RSA key by using some new secret factoring breakthrough. Perhaps so, but it is noteworthy that the U.S. government trusts the RSA algorithm enough in some cases to use it to protect its own nuclear weapons, according to Ron Rivest. And civilian academia has been intensively attacking it without success since 1978.

Perhaps the government has some classified methods of cracking the IDEA™ conventional encryption algorithm used in PGP. This is every cryptographer's worst nightmare. There can be no absolute security guarantees in practical cryptographic implementations.

Still, some optimism seems justified. The IDEA algorithm's designers are among the best cryptographers in Europe. It has had extensive security analysis and peer review from some of the best cryptanalysts in the unclassified world. It appears to have some design advantages over the DES in withstanding differential and linear cryptanalysis, which have both been used to crack the DES.

Besides, even if this algorithm has some subtle unknown weaknesses, PGP compresses the plaintext before encryption, which should greatly reduce those weaknesses. The computational workload to crack it is likely to be much more expensive than the value of the message.

If your situation justifies worrying about very formidable attacks of this caliber, then perhaps you should contact a data security consultant for some customized data security approaches tailored to your special needs. Boulder Software Engineering, whose address and phone are given in chapter 14, can provide such services.

In summary, without good cryptographic protection of your data communications, it may have been practically effortless and perhaps even routine for an opponent to intercept your messages, especially those sent through a modem or email system. If you use PGP and follow reasonable precautions, the attacker will have to expend far more effort and expense to violate your privacy.

If you protect yourself against the simplest attacks, and you feel confident that your privacy is not going to be violated by a determined and highly resourceful attacker, then you'll probably be safe using PGP. PGP gives you Pretty Good Privacy.

Legal Issues

Trademarks, Copyrights, and Warranties

"PGP", "Pretty Good Privacy", "Phil's Pretty Good Software", and the "Pretty Good" label for computer software and hardware products are all trademarks of Philip Zimmermann.

PGP and this manual are copyright by Philip Zimmermann. I reserve all rights, including but not limited to the right to make foreign language translations of the manual or the software and all derivative works of both.

MIT may have a copyright on the particular software distribution package that they distribute from the MIT FTP site. This copyright on the "compilation" of the distribution package in no way implies that MIT has a copyright on PGP itself, or its user documentation.

I assume no liability for damages resulting from the use of this software, even if the damage results from defects in this software, and make no representations concerning the merchantability of this software or its suitability for any specific purpose. It is provided "as is" without express or implied warranty of any kind. Because certain actions may delete files or render them unrecoverable, the author assumes no responsibility for the loss or modification of any data.

Patent Rights on the Algorithms

The RSA public key cryptosystem was developed at MIT, which holds a patent on it (U.S. patent #4,405,829, issued 20 Sep 1983).

A company in California called Public Key Partners (PKP) holds the exclusive commercial license to sell and sub-license the RSA public key cryptosystem. MIT distributes a freeware version of PGP under the terms of the RSAREF license from RSA Data Security, Inc. (RSADSI).

Non-U.S. users of earlier versions of PGP should note that the RSA patent does not apply outside the United States, and at least at the time of this writing, the author is not aware of any RSA patent in any other country. Federal agencies may use the RSA algorithm, because the government paid for the development of RSA with grants from the National Science Foundation and the Navy. But despite the fact of government users having free access to the RSA algorithm, government use of PGP has additional restrictions imposed by the agreement I have with ViaCrypt, as explained later.

I wrote my PGP software from scratch, with my own independently developed implementation of the RSA algorithm. Before publishing PGP in 1991, I got a formal written legal opinion from a patent attorney with extensive experience in software patents. I'm convinced that publishing PGP the way I did does not violate patent law.

Not only did PKP acquire the exclusive patent rights for the RSA cryptosystem, but they also acquired the exclusive rights to three other patents covering other public key schemes invented by others at Stanford University, also developed with federal funding. This one company claims to have a legal lock in the United States on nearly all practical public key cryptosystems. They even appear to be claiming patent rights on the very concept of public key cryptography, regardless of what clever new original algorithms are independently invented by others. I find such a comprehensive monopoly troubling, because I think public key cryptography is destined to become a crucial technology in the protection of our civil liberties and privacy in our increasingly connected society. At the very least, it places these vital tools at risk by affording to the government a single pressure point of influence.

Beginning with PGP version 2.5 (distributed by MIT, the holders of the original RSA patent), the freeware version of PGP uses the RSAREF subroutine library to perform its RSA calculations, under the RSAREF license, which allows noncommercial use in the

United States. RSAREF is a subroutine package from RSA Data Security Inc, that implements the RSA algorithm. The RSAREF subroutines are used instead of PGP's original subroutines to implement the RSA functions in PGP. See the RSAREF license for terms and conditions of use of RSAREF applications.

PGP 2.5 was released by MIT for a brief test period in May, 1994 before releasing 2.6. PGP 2.5 was released under the 16 March, 1994 RSAREF license, which is a perpetual license, so it may legally be used forever in the United States. But it would be better for PGP's legal and political future for users in the United States to upgrade to version 2.6 or later to facilitate the demise of PGP 2.3a and earlier versions. Also, PGP 2.5 has bugs that are corrected in 2.6, and 2.5 will not read the new data format after September 1, 1994. (See chapter 13.)

The PGP 2.0 release was a joint effort of an international team of software engineers, implementing enhancements to the original PGP with design guidance from me. It was released by Branko Lankester in The Netherlands and Peter Gutmann in New Zealand, out of reach of U.S. patent law. Although released only in Europe and New Zealand, it spontaneously spread to the United States without help from me or the PGP development team.

The IDEA™ conventional block cipher used by PGP is covered by a patent in Europe, held by ETH and a Swiss company called Ascom-Tech AG. The U.S. Patent number is 5,214,703, and the European patent number is EP 0 482 154 B1. IDEA™ is a trademark of Ascom-Tech AG. There is no license fee required for noncommercial use of IDEA. Commercial users of IDEA may obtain licensing details from Dieter Profos, Ascom Tech AG, Teleservices Section, Postfach 151, 4502 Solothurn, Switzerland, Tel +41 65 242885, Fax +41 65 235761.

Ascom-Tech AG has granted permission for the freeware version PGP to use the IDEA cipher in non-commercial uses, everywhere. In the United States and Canada, all commercial or government users must obtain a licensed version from ViaCrypt, who has a license from Ascom-Tech for the IDEA cipher.

Ascom-Tech has recently been changing its policies regarding the use of IDEA in PGP for commercial use outside the United States, and that policy still seems to be in flux. They tell me that their current thinking is as follows: They will allow commercial users of PGP outside the United States or Canada to use IDEA in PGP without paying royalties to Ascom-Tech, because it is not currently possible for commercial users to buy a licensed version of PGP outside the United States or Canada. If the legal situation in the United States changes in the future, so that users outside the United States or Canada can buy a licensed version of PGP (either from ViaCrypt, or from me, or from a foreign enterprise licensed by me), then Ascom-Tech will begin enforcing its patent licensing policies on commercial users who are in a position to buy a licensed version of PGP. To get a more up-to-date report on this, contact Ascom-Tech AG.

The ZIP compression routines in PGP come from freeware source code, with the author's permission. I'm not aware of any patents on the compression algorithms used in the ZIP routines.

Freeware Status and Restrictions

PGP is not shareware, it's freeware. Published as a community service. Giving PGP away for free will encourage far more people to use it, which will have a greater social impact. Feel free to disseminate the complete unmodified PGP release package as widely as possible, but be careful not to violate U.S. export controls if you live in the United States. Give it to all your friends. If you have access to any electronic Bulletin Board Systems, please upload the complete PGP executable object release package to as many BBS's as possible.

You may also disseminate the source code release package. PGP's source code is published to assist public scrutiny of PGP to show that it has no hidden weaknesses or back doors, and to help people to find bugs and report them. Recompile it and port it to new target machines. Experiment with the code and learn from it.

I place no restraints on your modifying the source code for your own use. However, do not distribute a modified version of PGP under the name "PGP" without first getting permission from me. Please respect this restriction. PGP's reputation for cryptographic integrity depends on maintaining strict quality control on PGP's cryptographic algorithms and protocols. Beyond that, ad hoc "improvements" to PGP can affect interoperability, which creates user confusion and compatability problems that could damage PGP's (and my own) reputation and undermine the good will earned by the PGP trademark.

This has already started to happen, which is why I'm making a point of it here. This creates technical support headaches, and I get phone calls from confused users who run into problems either because they have a mutant strain of PGP, or are trying to process a key, signature, or message that came from an incompatible mutant strain of PGP. The source code to PGP was not published to help spawn these mutant strains.

If you want to distribute a modified version of PGP, or use a modified version to send messages to other people, you should name the program in such a way that no one could mistake it for PGP. The messages, signatures, and keys it produces must also be labeled in such a way that no one could mistake them for material produced by PGP. If you feel you must modify your copy of PGP, and there is any chance that the modified version could escape into the environment, please contact me first to discuss some easy methods for how to prevent people from confusing your version with the standard PGP. Perhaps we'll even decide that your changes are appropriate for incorporating into the standard PGP release.

Also, you should note that official executable versions of PGP are always released signed by the PGP developers, so you can verify their authenticity. If you find a corrupted copy of PGP, or notice one being distributed, please contact the people doing the distribution and suggest that they replace this with an authentic version.

Some older versions of PGP were published under the terms of the General Public License (GPL), a license designed by the Free Software Foundation to protect the status of free software. Newer freeware versions of PGP are no longer published under the GPL. The RSAREF licensing terms are more stringent than those of the GPL. But even if a version of PGP is published without RSAREF, in a situation or place where the RSA patent does not apply, I still do not want the GPL to apply to PGP, for a variety of reasons, not the least of which is because the GPL is not optimal for protecting PGP from being republished with ad-hoc "improvements".

Outside the United States, the RSA patent is not in force, so PGP users there are free to use implementations of PGP that do not rely on RSAREF and its restrictions. Canadians may use PGP without using RSAREF, and there are legal ways to export PGP to Canada. In Canada, where RSAREF is not needed, it is easy to modify and recompile the current PGP source code to perform the RSA calculations without using the RSAREF library, just as it was done in PGP 2.3a. In such a case, this modified PGP may be re-released under the identical licensing terms as the current official freeware PGP release, but without the RSAREF-specific restrictions. It may not be re-released under the GPL, as certain older versions were. And this manual must accompany it. That modified version of PGP may not be used in environments where RSAREF would be needed.

Restrictions on Commercial Use of PGP

The freeware version of PGP is for personal, non-commercial use. For commercial use in the United States or Canada, contact ViaCrypt in Phoenix, Arizona (phone 602 944-0773, or email viacrypt@acm.org).

I made an agreement with ViaCrypt in the summer of 1993 to license the exclusive commercial rights to PGP, so that there would be a way for corporations to use PGP without risk of a patent infringement lawsuit from PKP. For PGP to succeed in the long term as a viable industry standard, the legal stigma associated with the RSA patent rights had to be resolved. ViaCrypt had already obtained a patent license from PKP to make, use, and sell products that practice the RSA patents. ViaCrypt offered a way out of the patent quagmire for PGP to penetrate the corporate environment. They could sell a fully-licensed version of PGP, but only if I licensed it to them under these terms. So we entered into an agreement to do that, opening the door for PGP's future in the commercial sector, which was necessary for PGP's long-term political future.

Therefore, regardless of the complexities and partially overlapping restrictions from all the other terms and conditions imposed by the various patent and copyright licenses (RSA, RSAREF, and IDEA) from various third parties, an additional overriding restriction on PGP usage is imposed by my own agreement with ViaCrypt: The freeware version of PGP is only for personal, non-commercial use—all other users in the United States and Canada must obtain a fully licensed version of PGP from ViaCrypt. The restrictions imposed by my agreement with ViaCrypt do not apply outside the United States or Canada.

Finally, if you want to turn PGP into a commercial product and make money selling it, then we must agree on a way for me to also make money on it. If you use PGP in such a manner that you must pay patent royalties or any other software licensing fees to the patent holders for any cryptographic algorithms used by PGP, then we must agree on a way for me to also be paid in some manner. Buying PGP from ViaCrypt is one way to meet this requirement.

Other Licensing Restrictions

Under no circumstances may PGP be distributed without the PGP documentation, including this *Official PGP User's Guide.* And, assuming this is an RSAREF version of PGP, the RSAREF license agreement must be kept with it. You must also keep the copyright, patent, and trademark notices on PGP and its documentation.

The standard freeware PGP release is primarily distributed in electronic form, as a single compressed archive file, containing a collection of files in a "shrink-wrapped" package. This package should not be broken up and the components separately distributed—in the interests of quality control, we want to make it difficult for users to obtain PGP without getting the full release package.

Distribution

In the United States, PGP is available for free from the Massachusetts Institute of Technology, under the restrictions described above.

The primary release site for PGP is the Massachusetts Institute of Technology, at their FTP site `net-dist.mit.edu`, in the `/pub/PGP` directory. You may obtain free copies or updates to PGP from this site, or any other Internet FTP site or BBS that PGP has spread to. Don't ask me for a copy directly from me, especially if you live outside the United States or Canada. I recommend that you not use any modified version of PGP that comes from any other source, other than MIT, ViaCrypt, or me, unless it is accompanied by a signed endorsement from me personally. You can get the official release software from many other distribution sites "downstream" from MIT. Hopefully, all these other sites are adhering to U.S. export controls.

The PGP version 2.6.2 executable object release package for MSDOS contains the PGP executable software, documentation, RSAREF license, sample key rings including my own public key, and signatures for the software and this manual, all in one PKZIP compressed file called 'pgp262.zip'. The PGP source release package for MSDOS contains all the C source files in one PKZIP compressed file called 'pgp262s.zip'. The filename for the release package is derived from the version number of the release.

Export Controls

The U.S. government has made it illegal in most cases to export good cryptographic technology, and that may include PGP. They regard this kind of software just like they regard munitions. This is determined not by legislation, but by administrative policies of the State Department, Defense Department and Commerce Department.

The U.S. government is using export restrictions as a means of suppressing both domestic and foreign availability of cryptographic technology. In particular, it is trying to suppress the emergence of an international standard for cryptographic protocols, until it can establish the Escrowed Encryption Standard (the Clipper chip) as the dominant standard.

Any export restrictions on PGP are imposed by the U.S. government. This does not imply that I or MIT agree with these restrictions. We just comply with them. We do not impose additional licensing restrictions of our own on the use of PGP outside of the United States, other than those restrictions that already apply inside the United States. PGP may be subject to export controls. Anyone wishing to export it should first consult the State Department's Office of Defense Trade Controls.

I will not export this software out of the United States or Canada in cases when it is illegal to do so under U.S. controls, and I urge other people not to export it on their own. If you live outside the United States or Canada, I urge you not to violate U.S. export laws by getting any version of PGP in a way that violates those laws. Since thousands of domestic users got the first version after its initial publication, it somehow leaked out of the United States and spread itself widely abroad, like dandelion seeds blowing in the wind.

Starting with PGP version 2.0 through version 2.3a, the release point of the software has been outside the United States, on publicly-accessible computers in Europe. Each release was electronically sent back into the United States and posted on publicly-accessible computers in the United States by PGP privacy activists in foreign countries. There are some restrictions in the United States regarding the import of munitions, but I'm not aware of any cases where this was ever enforced for importing cryptographic software into the United States. I imagine that a legal action of that type would be quite a spectacle of controversy.

ViaCrypt PGP is sold in the United States and Canada and is not for export. The following language was supplied by the U.S. government to ViaCrypt for inclusion in the ViaCrypt PGP documentation:

PGP is export restricted by the Office of Export Administration, United States Department of Commerce and the Offices of Defense Trade Controls and Munitions Control, United States Department of State. PGP cannot be exported or reexported, directly or indirectly, (a) without all export or reexport licenses and governmental approvals required by any applicable laws, or (b) in violation of any prohibition against the export or reexport of any part of PGP.

The government may take the position that the freeware PGP versions are also subject to those controls.

The freeware PGP versions 2.5 and 2.6 were released through a posting on a controlled FTP site maintained by MIT. This site has restrictions and limitations which have been used on other FTP sites to comply with export control requirements with respect to other encryption software such as Kerberos and software from RSA Data Security, Inc. I urge you not to do anything which would weaken those controls or facilitate any improper export of PGP.

Although PGP has become a worldwide de facto standard for email encryption, and is widely available overseas, I still get calls from people outside the United States who ask me if it is legal to use it in their own country, for versions that are already available there. Please don't contact me to ask me if it is legal to use PGP in your country if you live outside the United States. That question is not up to me. I've got enough legal problems of my own with export control issues, without getting involved in giving you legal advice over my phone. It might even put me at some legal risk to simply answer a question like that for a foreigner. If this question concerns you, ask someone else, like a lawyer.

You may have a need to use PGP in a commercial application outside the United States or Canada. Unfortunately, at the time of this writing, there is no current commercial source for PGP outside the United States or Canada. I am trying to find a U.S.-legal way to make a commercially licensed version available abroad, but right now the U.S. export restrictions make that difficult without putting me at legal risk. This situation may change.

Some foreign governments impose serious penalties on anyone inside their country for merely using encrypted communications. In some countries they might even shoot you for that. But if you live in that kind of country, perhaps you need PGP even more.

My Legal Situation

At the time of this writing, I am the target of a U.S. Customs criminal investigation in the Northern District of California. A criminal investigation is not a civil lawsuit. Civil lawsuits do not involve prison terms. My defense attorney has been told by the Assistant U.S. Attorney that the area of law of interest to the investigation has to do with the export controls on encryption software. The federal mandatory sentencing guidelines for this offense are 41 to 51 months in a federal prison. U.S. Customs appears to be taking the position that electronic domestic publication of encryption software is the same as exporting it. The prosecutor has issued a number of federal grand jury subpoenas. It may be months before a decision is reached on whether to seek indictment. This situation may change at any time, so this description may be out of date by the time you read it. Watch the news for further developments. If I am indicted and this goes to trial, it will be a major test case.

I have a legal defense fund set up for this case. So far, no other organization is doing the fundraising for me, so I am depending on people like you to contribute directly to this cause. If you care about the future of your civil liberties in the information age, then perhaps you will care about this case. The legal fees are expensive, the meter is running, and I need your help. The fund is run by my lead defense attorney, Phil Dubois, here in Boulder. Please send your contributions to:

Philip L. Dubois, Lawyer
2305 Broadway
Boulder, Colorado 80304 USA
Phone (303) 444-3885
Email: dubois@csn.org

You can also phone in your donation and put it on a credit card. If you want to be really cool, you can use Internet email to send in your contribution, encrypting your message with PGP so that no one can intercept your credit card number. Include in your email message your Mastercard or Visa number, expiration date, name on the card, and amount of donation. Then sign it with your own key and encrypt it with Phil Dubois's public key (his key is included in the standard PGP distribution package, in the 'keys.asc' file). Put a note on the subject line that this is a donation to my legal defense fund, so that Mr. Dubois will decrypt it promptly. Please don't send a lot of casual encrypted email to him. I'd rather he use his valuable time to work on my case.

If you want to read some press stories to find out why this is an important case, see the following references:

1. William Bulkeley, "Cipher Probe", *Wall Street Journal*, 28 April 1994, front page.

2. John Cary, "Spy vs. Computer Nerd: The Fight Over Data Security", *Business Week*, 4 October 1993, page 43.

3. Jon Erickson, "Cryptography Fires Up the Feds", *Dr. Dobb's Journal*, December 1993, page 6.

4. John Markoff, "Federal Inquiry on Software Examines Privacy Programs", *New York Times*, 21 September 1993, page C1.

5. Kurt Kleiner, "Punks and Privacy", *Mother Jones Magazine*, January/February 1994, page 17.

6. Steven Levy, "Battle of the Clipper Chip", *New York Times Magazine*, 12 June 1994, page 44.

7. Steven Levy, "Crypto Rebels", *WIRED*, May/June 1993, page 54.

8. John Markoff, "Cyberspace Under Lock and Key", *New York Times*, 13 February 1994.

9. Philip Elmer-DeWitt, "Who Should Keep the Keys", *Time*, 14 March 1994, page 90.

There are a great many other articles on PGP from around the world. I'm keeping a scrapbook.

13

Compatibility with Previous and Future Versions of PGP

PGP version 2.6 can read anything produced by versions 2.3 through 2.7. However, because of a negotiated agreement between MIT and RSA Data Security, PGP 2.6 was programmed to change its behavior slightly on 1 September 1994, triggered by a built-in software timer. On that date, version 2.6 started producing a new and slightly different data format for messages, signatures and keys. PGP 2.6 will still be able to read and process messages, signatures, and keys produced under the old format, but it will generate the new format. This change is intended to discourage people from continuing to use the older (2.3a and earlier) versions of PGP, which Public Key Partners contends infringes its RSA patent (see chapter 12). ViaCrypt PGP (see the section "Where to Get a Commercial Version of PGP" in chapter 14), versions 2.4 and 2.7, avoids questions of infringement through Viacrypt's license arrangement with Public Key Partners. PGP 2.5 and 2.6 avoid questions of infringement by using the RSAREF™ Cryptographic Toolkit, under license from RSA Data Security, Inc.

Outside the United States, the RSA patent is not in force, so PGP users there are free to use implementations of PGP that do not rely on RSAREF and its restrictions. See the notes on foreign versions in chapter 12. It seems likely that any versions of PGP prepared outside the United States will accept the new format, whose detailed description is available from MIT. If everyone upgrades before September 1994, or soon thereafter, there will be little interoperability problems.

This format change beginning with 2.6 is similar to the process that naturally happens when new features are added, causing older versions of PGP to be unable to read stuff from the newer PGP, while the newer version can still read the old stuff. The only difference is that this is a "legal upgrade", instead of a technical one. It's a worthwhile change, if it can achieve peace in our time.

According to ViaCrypt, which sells a commercial version of PGP, ViaCrypt PGP will evolve to maintain interoperability with new freeware versions of PGP.

There is a another change that affects interoperability with earlier versions of PGP. Unfortunately, due to data format limitations imposed by RSAREF, PGP 2.5 and 2.6 cannot interpret any messages or signatures made with PGP version 2.2 or earlier. Since we had no choice but to use the new data formats, because of the need to switch to RSAREF, we can't do anything about this problem.

Beginning with version 2.4 (which was ViaCrypt's first version) through at least 2.6, PGP does not allow you to generate RSA keys bigger than 1024 bits. The upper limit was always intended to be 1024 bits (there had to be some kind of upper limit, for performance and interoperability reasons). But because of a bug in earlier versions of PGP, it was possible to generate keys larger than 1024 bits. These larger keys caused interoperability problems between different older versions of PGP that used different arithmetic algorithms with different native word sizes. On some platforms, PGP choked on the larger keys. In addition to these older key size problems, the 1024-bit limit was enforced by RSAREF. Even though a 1024-bit key is very likely to be well out of reach of attacks by major governments, starting with version 2.6.2, PGP supports 2048-bit keys.

In general, there is compatibility from version 2.0 upwards through 2.4. Because new features are added, older versions may not always be able to handle some files created with newer versions. Because of massive changes to all the algorithms and data structures, PGP version 2.0 (and later) is not even slightly compatible with PGP version 1.0, which no one uses anymore anyway.

Future versions of PGP may have to change the data formats for messages, signatures, keys and key rings, in order to provide important new features. We will endeavor to make future versions handle keys, signatures, and messages from this version, but this is not guaranteed. Future releases may provide conversion utilities to convert old keys, but you may have to dispose of old messages created with the old PGP. Also, this current version may not be able to read stuff produced by all future versions.

Sources of Information on PGP

Where to Get the Freeware Version of PGP

The Massachusetts Institute of Technology distributes version 2.6 of PGP within the United States only. It is available from net-dist.mit.edu, a controlled FTP site that has restrictions and limitations, similar to those used by RSA Data Security, Inc., to comply with export control requirements. The software resides in the directory /pub/PGP.

A reminder: Set mode to binary or image when doing an FTP transfer. And when doing a kermit download to your PC, specify 8-bit binary mode at both ends.

There are two compressed archive files in the standard release, with the file name derived from the release version number. For PGP version 2.6.2, you must get 'pgp262.zip' which contains the MSDOS binary executable and the PGP User's Guide, and you can optionally get 'pgp262s.zip' which contains all the source code. These files can be decompressed with the MSDOS shareware archive decompression utility PKUNZIP.EXE, version 1.10 or later. For Unix users who lack an implementation of UNZIP, the source code can also be found in the compressed tar file 'pgp262s.tar.Z'.

If you don't have any local BBS phone numbers handy, here is a BBS you might try. The Catacombs BBS, operated by Mike Johnson in Longmont, Colorado, has PGP available for download by people in the United States or Canada only. The BBS phone number is (303) 772-1062. Mike Johnson's voice phone number is (303) 772-1773, and his email address is mpj@csn.org. Mike also has PGP available on an Internet FTP site for users in the United States or Canada only; the site name is `csn.org`, in directory '`/mpj`', and you must read the '`README.MPJ`' file to get it.

Here are a few people and their email addresses or phone numbers you can contact in some countries to get information on local PGP availability for versions earlier than 2.5:

Jean-loup Gailly
`jloup@chorus.fr`
France

Peter Gutmann
`pgut1@cs.aukuni.ac.nz`
New Zealand

Hugh Kennedy
`70042.710@compuserve.com`
Germany

Branko Lankester
`branko@hacktic.nl`
+31 2159 42242
The Netherlands

Where to Get a Commercial Version of PGP

To get a fully licensed version of PGP for use in the United States or Canada, contact:

ViaCrypt
9033 North 24th Avenue, Suite 7
Phoenix, Arizona 85021 USA
Phone: (602) 944-0773, or (800) 536-2664
Fax: (602) 943-2601
Email: `viacrypt@acm.org`

ViaCrypt has a version of PGP for MSDOS and a number of Unix platforms. They also have a Windows shell version, and other versions are under development, including Macintosh. If you have a need to use PGP in a commercial or government setting, and ViaCrypt has a version of PGP for your hardware platform, you should get ViaCrypt PGP.

ViaCrypt has obtained all the necessary licenses from PKP, Ascom-Tech AG, and Philip Zimmermann to sell PGP for use in commercial or government environments. ViaCrypt PGP is every bit as secure as the freeware PGP, and is entirely compatible in both directions with the freeware version of PGP. ViaCrypt PGP is the perfect way to get a fully licensed version of PGP into your corporate environment.

If you work in a large company and you are a fan of PGP, I urge you to try to persuade your company to buy lots of copies of PGP from ViaCrypt. Not just because that will earn royalties for me. If ViaCrypt can make PGP a commercial success, it will go a long way toward cementing PGP's political future as an unstoppable standard for email encryption in the corporate world. The corporate world is where the money is, and that affects public policy like nothing else. And that includes government policy to suppress strong cryptography.

Reporting PGP Bugs

Bugs in PGP should be reported via email to MIT, which is the official distribution site. The address for bug reports is pgp-bugs@mit.edu. MIT will forward a copy of your bug report to me. When you report bugs, be sure to specify what machine and operating system you are using and what version of PGP you have, and provide enough detail to reproduce the problem. It would also be a good idea to find out if you have the latest version of PGP, in case the bug has already been fixed. Also, it's a good idea to make sure it really is a bug before you report it. RTFM.

Fan Mail, Updates, and News

After all this work I have to admit I wouldn't mind getting some fan mail for PGP, to gauge its popularity. Let me know what you think about it and how many of your friends use it. Suggestions for enhancing PGP are welcome, too. Perhaps a future PGP release will reflect your suggestions.

This project has not been funded and the project has nearly eaten me alive. This means you usually won't get a reply to your mail, unless you only need a short written reply and you include a stamped self-addressed envelope. But I often do reply to email. Please keep it in English, as my foreign language skills are weak. If you call and I'm not in, it's best to just try again later. I usually don't return long distance phone calls, unless you leave a message that I can call you collect, and even then I might not return your call. If you need any significant amount of my time, I am available on a paid consulting basis, and I always return those calls.

The most inconvenient mail I get is for some well-intentioned person to send me a few dollars asking me for a copy of PGP. I don't send it to them because I'd rather avoid any legal problems with PKP. Or worse, sometimes these requests are from foreign countries, and I would be risking a violation of U.S. cryptographic export control laws. Even if there were no legal hassles involved in sending PGP to them, they usually don't send enough money to make it worth my time. I'm just not set up as a low cost low volume mail order business. I can't just ignore the request and keep the money, because they probably regard the money as a fee for me to fulfill their request. If I return the money, I might have to get in my car and drive down to the post office and buy some postage stamps, because these requests rarely include a stamped self-addressed envelope. And I have to take the time to write a polite reply that I can't do it. If I postpone the reply and set the letter down on my desk, it might be buried within minutes and won't see the light of day again for months. Multiply these minor inconveniences by the number of requests I get, and you can see the problem. Isn't it enough that the software is free? It would be nicer if people could try to get PGP from any of the myriad other sources. If you don't have a modem, ask a friend to get it for you.

If anyone wants to volunteer to improve PGP, please let me know. It could certainly use some more work. Some features were deferred to get it out the door. A number of PGP users have since donated their time to port PGP to Unix on Sun SPARCstations, to Ultrix, to VAX/VMS, to OS/2, to the Amiga, and to the Atari ST. Perhaps you can help port it to some new environments. But please let me know if you plan to port or add enhancements to PGP, to avoid duplication of effort, and to avoid starting with an obsolete version of the source code.

Because so many foreign language translations of PGP have been produced, most of them are not distributed with the regular PGP release package because it would require too much disk space. Separate language translation "kits" are available from a number of independent sources, and are sometimes available separately from the same distribution centers that carry the regular PGP release software. These kits include translated versions of the file 'LANGUAGE.TXT', 'PGP.HLP', and the *Official PGP User's Guide*. If you want to produce a translation for your own native language, contact me first to get the latest information and standard guidelines, and to find out if it's been translated to your language already. To find out where to get a foreign language kit for your language, you might check on the Internet newsgroups, or get it from Mike Johnson (mpj@csn.org).

If you have access to the Internet, watch for announcements of new releases of PGP on the Internet newsgroups 'sci.crypt' and PGP's own newsgroup, 'alt.security.pgp'.

To Contact the Author

The author is a software engineer/consultant with 19 years experience, specializing in embedded real-time systems, cryptography, authentication, key management protocols, and data communications. I am available to work on custom versions of cryptography and authentication products, as well as custom product development services. My firm's address is:

Boulder Software Engineering
3021 Eleventh Street
Boulder, Colorado 80304 USA
Phone: (303) 541-0140 (10:00 am–7:00 pm Mountain Time)
Fax: arrange by phone
Internet: prz@acm.org

Computer-Related Political Groups

PGP is a very political piece of software. It seems appropriate to mention here some computer-related activist groups. Full details on these groups, and how to join them, is provided in a separate document file in the PGP release package.

The Electronic Privacy Information Center (EPIC) is a public interest research center in Washington, DC. It was established in 1994 to focus public attention on emerging privacy issues relating to the National Information Infrastructure, such as the Clipper Chip, the Digital Telephony proposal, medical record privacy, and the sale of consumer data. EPIC is sponsored by the Fund for Constitutional Government and Computer Professionals for Social Responsibility. EPIC publishes the EPIC Alert and EPIC Reports, pursues Freedom of Information Act litigation, and conducts policy research on emerging privacy issues. For more information email info@epic.org, or contact them at

EPIC
666 Pennsylvania Ave., SE, Suite 301
Washington, DC 20003
(202) 544-9240 (tel)
(202) 547-5482 (fax)

The Electronic Frontier Foundation (EFF) was founded in 1990 to assure freedom of expression in digital media, with a particular emphasis on applying the principles embodied in the U.S. Constitution and the Bill of Rights to computer-based communication. They can be reached in Washington DC, at (202) 861-7700; their email address is eff@eff.org.

Computer Professionals For Social Responsibility (CPSR) encourages computer professionals and computer users to advocate for the responsible use of information technology and empowers all who use computer technology to participate in public policy debates on the impacts of computers on society. They can be reached in Palo Alto, California, at (415) 322-3778; their email address is cpsr@csli.stanford.edu.

The League for Programming Freedom (LPF) is a grass-roots organization of professors, students, businessmen, programmers and users dedicated to bringing back the freedom to write programs. They regard patents on computer algorithms as harmful to the U.S. software industry (and so do I!). They can be reached at (617) 433-7071; their email address is lpf@uunet.uu.net.

Recommended Readings

1. Bruce Schneier, *Applied Cryptography: Protocols, Algorithms, and Source Code in C,* John Wiley & Sons, 1993 (a watershed work on the subject.)

2. Dorothy Denning, *Cryptography and Data Security,* Addison-Wesley, 1982

3. Dorothy Denning, "Protecting Public Keys and Signature Keys", *IEEE Computer,* February 1983

4. Martin E. Hellman, "The Mathematics of Public-Key Cryptography," *Scientific American,* August 1979

5. Steven Levy, "Crypto Rebels", *WIRED,* May/June 1993, page 54 (a "must-read" article on PGP and other related topics)

6. Steven Levy, "Battle of the Clipper Chip", *New York Times Magazine,* 12 June 1994, page 44 (great article, great photos.)

7. William Bulkeley, "Cipher Probe", *Wall Street Journal,* 28 April 1994, page 1

The following are for readers who want more detail:

8. Ronald Rivest, "The MD5 Message Digest Algorithm", MIT Laboratory for Computer Science, 1991

9. Xuejia Lai, *On the Design and Security of Block Ciphers,* ETH Series on Information Processing (Ed. J. L. Massey), Vol. 1, Hartung-Gorre Verlag, Konstanz, Switzerland, 1992

10. Philip Zimmermann, "A Proposed Standard Format for RSA Cryptosystems", in *Advances in Computer Security,* Vol III, edited by Rein Turn, Artech House, 1988

11. Paul Wallich, "Electronic Envelopes", *Scientific American,* February 1993, page 30. (An article on PGP)

12. William Stallings, "Pretty Good Privacy", *BYTE,* July 1994, page 193

13. Philip Zimmermann, *PGP Source Code and Internals,* MIT Press, 1995

Appendix
PGP Quick Reference

Basic Commands

To encrypt a plaintext file with the recipient's public key:

`pgp -e` *textfile her_userid*

To sign a plaintext file with your secret key:

`pgp -s` *textfile* `[-u` *your_userid]*

To sign a plaintext ASCII text file with your secret key, producing a signed plaintext message suitable for sending via E-mail:

`pgp -sta` *textfile* `[-u` *your_userid]*

To sign a plaintext file with your secret key, and then encrypt it with the recipient's public key:

`pgp -es` *textfile her_userid* `[-u` *your_userid]*

To encrypt a plaintext file with just conventional cryptography:

`pgp -c` *textfile*

To decrypt an encrypted file, or to check the signature integrity of a signed file:

pgp *ciphertextfile* [-o *plaintextfile*]

To encrypt a message for any number of multiple recipients:

pgp -e *textfile userid1 userid2 userid3*

Key Management Commands

To generate your own unique public/secret key pair:

pgp -kg

To add a public or secret key file's contents to your public or secret key ring:

pgp -ka *keyfile* [keyring]

To extract (copy) a key from your public or secret key ring:

pgp -kx *userid keyfile* [*keyring*]

or:

pgp -kxa *userid keyfile* [*keyring*]

To view the contents of your public key ring:

pgp -kv[v] [*userid*] [*keyring*]

To view the "fingerprint" of a public key, to help verify it over the telephone with its owner:

pgp -kvc [*userid*] [*keyring*]

To view the contents and check the certifying signatures of your public key ring:

pgp -kc [*userid*] [*keyring*]

To edit the userid or pass phrase for your secret key:

pgp -ke *userid* [*keyring*]

To edit the trust parameters for a public key:

pgp -ke *userid* [*keyring*]

To remove a key or just a userid from your public key ring:

pgp -kr *userid* [*keyring*]

To sign and certify someone else's public key on your public key ring:

pgp -ks *her_userid* [-u *your_userid*] [*keyring*]

To remove selected signatures from a userid on a keyring:

pgp -krs *userid* [*keyring*]

To permanently revoke your own key, issuing a key compromise certificate:

pgp -kd *your_userid*

To disable or reenable a public key on your own public key ring:

pgp -kd *userid*

Esoteric Commands

To decrypt a message and leave the signature on it intact:

pgp -d *ciphertextfile*

To create a signature certificate that is detached from the document:

pgp -sb *textfile* [-u *your_userid*]

To detach a signature certificate from a signed message:

pgp -b *ciphertextfile*

Command Options That Can Be Used in Combination with Other Command Options (Sometimes Even Spelling Interesting Words!)

To produce a ciphertext file in ASCII radix-64 format, just add the '-a' option when encrypting or signing a message or extracting a key:

pgp -sea *textfile her_userid*

or:

pgp -kxa *userid keyfile* [keyring]

To wipe out the plaintext file after producing the ciphertext file, just add the '-w' (wipe) option when encrypting or signing a message:

pgp -sew *message.txt her_userid*

To specify that a plaintext file contains ASCII text, not binary, and should be converted to recipient's local text line conventions, add the '-t' (text) option to other options:

pgp -seat *message.txt her_userid*

To view the decrypted plaintext output on your screen (like the Unix-style more command), without writing it to a file, use the '-m' (more) option while decrypting:

pgp -m *ciphertextfile*

To specify that the recipient's decrypted plaintext will be shown *only* on her screen and cannot be saved to disk, add the '-m' option:

pgp -steam *message.txt her_userid*

To recover the original plaintext filename while decrypting, add the '-p' option:

pgp -p *ciphertextfile*

To use a Unix-style filter mode, reading from standard input and writing to standard output, add the '-f' option:

pgp -feast *her_userid* < *inputfile* > *outputfile*

Index